# UNDERSTANDING
# ASSET
# ALLOCATION

# UNDERSTANDING ASSET ALLOCATION

## Scott Frush

**McGraw-Hill**

New York  Chicago  San Francisco  Lisbon  London
Madrid  Mexico City  Milan  New Delhi
San Juan  Seoul  Singapore
Sydney  Toronto

The *McGraw·Hill* Companies

1 2 3 4 5 6 7 8 9 0   FGR/FGR   0 9 8 7 6

ISBN-13: 978-0-07-147594-5
ISBN-10: 0-07-147594-X

This publication is designed to provide accurate and authoritative information in regard to the subject matter covered. It is sold with the understanding that neither the author nor the publisher is engaged in rendering legal, accounting, or other professional service. If legal advice or other expert assistance is required, the services of a competent professional person should be sought.
—*From a declaration of principles jointly adopted by a committee of the American Bar Association and a committee of publishers.*

This book is printed on acid-free paper.

McGraw-Hill books are available at special quantity discounts to use as premiums and sales promotions, or for use in corporate training programs. For more information, please write to the Director of Special Sales, Professional Publishing, McGraw-Hill, Two Penn Plaza, New York, NY 10121-2298. Or contact your local bookstore.

**Library of Congress Cataloging-in-Publication Data**

Frush, Scott P.
    Understanding asset allocation / by Scott P. Frush.
        p.   cm.
    Includes index.
    ISBN 0-07-147594-X (pbk. : alk. paper)
    1. Asset allocation. 2. Portfolio management. 3. Investments. I. Title.
    HG4529.5.F79 2006
    332.6—dc22                                                  2006006789

*To my wonderful parents*

# Contents

# Acknowledgments

My sincere thanks to so many people who were instrumental in making this book happen. Special thanks to my wife, Christina, for her unwavering support, time, and patience. Thank you to Mark Waugh, John Northcott, Michael Dudkowski, Timothy Hutton, Jason Frush, Howard Katz, Rich Mazel, Jennifer Rass, and Scott Theiring for your significant contributions and unique insights. Your help is much appreciated!

I am particularly thankful to Stephen Isaacs at McGraw-Hill for his vision and commitment to publishing this book. I wish to thank Gini Graham Scott of Creative Communications and Research for helping in the prestages of publishing this book. Special appreciation to Mario, John, and Michael Fallone of Cantoro's Italian Market for their support and assistance.

I'd be remiss if I did not thank James Miller, John Nixon, Ronald Miller, Jeff Buric, Jay Fishman, Frank D. Stella, and Brian Lohr. These people impacted my life greatly and were instrumental in my career pursuit and advancement in the field of investments and financial management.

With sincere appreciation for their assistance in many different ways, I wish to thank the hardworking and friendly staff at Barnes and Noble of Livonia, Michigan, and Borders of Novi, Michigan. For professional peer review, thanks to Chad Sharliper of Rather & Kittrell Capital Management, David Huff of Mathew Person, CPA, and Michael Kitces of Pinnacle Advisory Group. Thanks to Steve Wadle for hosting my first ever book signing event. Sincere thanks to my advisory board at Frush Financial Group for their driving force and masterful tutelage.

Most of all, thank you to all of my clients for giving me the opportunity to not only do what I love but also for allowing me to make a difference in your lives. I am truly blessed to be a part of the lives of so many special people.

# Introduction

Every day fortunes are made and every day fortunes are lost. What separates the two is the pursuit and implementation of proper investment planning and steadfast resolve to see it through. From boom-to-bust cycles to corporate scandals, the need to protect and grow wealth the right way has never been more obvious or more critical. Experience and research have demonstrated firsthand that asset allocation is the right way.

The vision of this book is to help investors achieve and exceed their financial goals and objectives and live the life they dream. Every good vision must have a mission to make it happen. The mission of this book is to teach investors how to design, implement, and manage an optimal portfolio for long-term results. To accomplish this mission, investors must work at it each day because there are no shortcuts. Employing proper asset allocation is easy to envision, simple to commence, yet significantly difficult to sustain over time. There are many hurdles and challenges to overcome. To the victor go the spoils.

*Understanding Asset Allocation* was written to accomplish this mission and overcome any challenges you may encounter. It uses a commonsense, step-by-step, and logical approach for you to accomplish the mission. By committing yourself to a proven investment strategy, you will build a portfolio with less risk and yet experience higher investment performance over time. Asset allocation is an intrinsic part of this proven investment philosophy. The investment strategy of asset allocation is to help you earn the highest total return for the least amount of portfolio risk. As a result, asset allocation helps you avoid market timing and painful security selection and provides the most promising framework for the long term.

The target audience for this book is novice to intermediate investors; however, given the breadth of material, those with advanced knowledge will learn new things as well. The single directive of this book is to explain in simple language and easy to understand terms the most important aspects of what asset allocation is and how best to employ it. As a result, this book will not get into the nitty-gritty or complex mathematics of asset allocation. Those topics can be reviewed once a solid understanding of the fundamentals is learned. Chapter 16 provides suggestions for a number of books that really get into the advanced topics.

## Before We Get Started

Time and time again I tell people to *manage your portfolio before it manages you*. Managing your portfolio always begins with you. Never rely on someone else to do what you should be doing. Many small business owners tell me that no one cares like the owner. The same can be said for your portfolio. When it comes to your investments, you really have two options: accomplish those tasks that will help you manage your portfolio or simply forgo them and let your portfolio manage you. Since you are already reading this book, you have demonstrated your willingness to be proactive with managing your portfolio. Consider this book an invaluable tool to help you with your endeavor.

This book is based on my experiences of working directly with individual clients and performing in-depth research for over a decade. I highly encourage you to work your way through this book from page 1, embracing the help and suggestions provided and putting them to work for you.

## What's in Your Golf Bag?

What kind of clubs do you bring and use when you golf? Do you bring all drivers? How about all putters? What about all woods? If you brought all drivers you would probably do well at the beginning of your game, but then things would fall apart on the greens or if you were unlucky enough to hit into a sand trap. Conversely, if you stocked your golf bag with all putters it would probably take you a horrific number of swings to get from the tee to the green. The golf ranger would undoubtedly kick you off the course (permanently, I might add) for even trying.

Given these monumental challenges, would you ever use just one type of club for an entire round of golf? Of course you wouldn't; that would be truly and utterly foolish. The same concept can be applied to your investment portfolio. When allocating your portfolio, it is foolish to use only equity investments or fixed-income investments. As does each type of golf club have a place in your golf bag, so too do different asset classes have a place in your investment portfolio.

You're not a golfer, you say. How about chess? Can you play with all pawns? How about football? Can you field a team with all punters or quarterbacks? For those who don't play sports, can you host a dinner party and only provide forks and serve one type of food to your guests?

Regardless of the task, to be successful you need a full arsenal of tools at your disposal. This book will introduce you to all of the asset allocation tools you will need to get the job done right and be successful at it.

## My Guiding Principles and Your Learning Outcomes

When writing *Understanding Asset Allocation* I did so by adhering to a number of guiding principles so that novice and intermediate investors would have everything they need to know about asset allocation to build a winning portfolio in bull and bear markets. Regardless of whether we are discussing what asset allocation is, how to draft and implement your plan, or how to maintain and grow your portfolio, each was adhered to with resolve. These guiding principles are as follows:

- Investors want to understand the terminology and how asset allocation is beneficial.
- Investors want to feel secure and in control of their investment portfolio.
- Investors want to protect their investment portfolio from large swings in market value.
- Investors want to achieve both their preretirement and retirement financial goals.
- Investors want to be knowledgeable on the subject of asset allocation.
- Investors want to read a step-by-step guide rather than a textbook full of technical jargon.
- Investors want to learn *what not* to do as much as they want to learn *what* to do.

*Understanding Asset Allocation* is written for those investors who want to allocate their portfolios properly for solid long-term portfolio performance. It is critical that asset allocation be appropriate and suitable for each and every investor. This book will assist investors with determining their optimal asset allocations and managing their portfolios the right way over time. As such, the following are the seven goals of this book to ensure you learn everything you need to know about asset allocation.

- Understand the basics of asset allocation
- Understand the important relationship between risk and return
- Understand the fundamentals of each asset class
- Understand how to manage your portfolio with asset allocation
- Understand investor behavior and asset allocation pitfalls
- Understand how risk profile, time horizon, goals, and needs impact portfolios
- Understand how to make asset allocation work for you from this point forward

## Not Everyone Plays Golf

Each and every investor is different. One type of portfolio is not going to work for everyone. Although my guiding principles afforded me the opportunity to speak to the masses, some topics will not be applicable to all investors. For example, the model portfolios in Part Three are based on the age of the investor. Thus, the chapter for early accumulators is not exactly applicable for older investors. Depending on your situation, some material in this book may be more relevant or some less relevant. As a result, you may want to reread some material and skim other material. In addition, some highlights may be more appropriate for you and some may not. Exercise care, skill, and patience when reading the material and applying it to your personal situation.

## How to Get the Most from this Book

*Understanding Asset Allocation* is divided into four parts. No one part is of greater importance than the others. All parts are of equal value. Consequently, reading this book from Chapter 1 to Chapter 16 is your best route. The book is structured to provide maximum benefit, ease of learning, and quick and simple referencing. As such, the book begins with a discussion of the fundamentals of asset allocation and is followed by a discussion of the asset classes, the building blocks of successful investing. Part Three shows how to put into motion what the two opening parts discussed. The final content helps to reinforce and enhance the preceding material.

# A Review of the Chapters

Part One is all about the basics and theory of asset allocation. Chapter 1 leads off with a discussion of why asset allocation is so important and what are the benefits. Chapter 2 is about two of the most important concepts with investing: investment risk and return. The third chapter handles all of the fundamentals of asset allocation while the final chapter in Part One talks about the 10 cornerstone principles of asset allocation.

The second part of this book focuses on the asset class alternatives. Accordingly, Chapter 5 discusses equity investments. Chapter 6 follows this lead and discusses fixed-income investments. Chapters 7 and 8 touch on alternative investments and global investments, respectively.

Part Three begins the application phase. This part focuses on determining and managing your asset allocation. As such, Chapter 9 provides a solid discussion of multi-asset-class portfolios while Chapter 10 builds on this by discussing asset allocation plans for winning portfolios. The next three chapters each take a specific age group and provide model portfolios most appropriate for their unique situation.

Part Four is all about some peripheral topics of asset allocation. Chapter 14 discusses the leading misconceptions and common mistakes of asset allocation. Chapter 15 complements the preceding chapter by providing a snapshot of the many behavioral blunders investors sometimes make that have the potential of sabotaging their asset allocation. The final chapter talks about the value of professional help with investing and provides resources for evaluating and seeking out additional help.

# UNDERSTANDING
# ASSET
# ALLOCATION

# PART ONE

# WHAT YOU NEED TO KNOW FIRST

C H A P T E R

1

# Importance and Benefits of Asset Allocation

## The Holy Grail of Investing?

Numerous landmark research studies have concluded that *how* you allocate your assets, rather than *which* individual investments you select or *when* you buy or sell them, is the leading determinant of investment performance over time. Not stock picking, not market timing, not the latest and greatest hot investment without risk. Of course this does not mean that asset allocation is the holy grail of investing, but it surely is the next best thing. Nothing else comes close. If there were something more powerful, I would be writing about it.

The key to a lifetime of investment success is not complex or difficult to understand or apply. But rather, asset allocation is simple and straightforward. The essence of asset allocation is all about gaining and maintaining an edge that will promote long-term investment performance and ensure your financial independence, control, and security. Unfortunately, as you will see from research and real-world results, many investors do not employ proper asset allocation, let alone know what it is really all about.

3

If I have noticed anything over these 60 years on Wall Street, it is that people do not succeed in forecasting what's going to happen to the stock market.

—*BENJAMIN GRAHAM*

*Asset allocation* is best described as dividing your investment portfolio and other investable money into different asset classes. The concept underlying the allocation of your portfolio in such a way is that by splitting your investment portfolio into different asset classes, you will reduce portfolio risk and enhance your long-term risk-adjusted return. In other words, asset allocation provides you with your best opportunity to earn solid returns over time while assuming the level of portfolio risk most suitable for your unique situation. The allocation of your assets is based on a number of very important factors, such as current financial position, investment time horizon, level of wealth, financial goals and obligations, and risk profile. A few other variables, or portfolio allocation inputs as I like to call them, are discussed at length later in this book. Specifically, the three most important inputs that determine your asset allocation are your financial objectives and needs, your investment time horizon, and your risk profile. To build an optimal portfolio, your unique risk profile is of utmost importance. Your risk profile includes three variables: your tolerance for risk, your capacity for risk, and your need to assume risk. We'll get into a more detailed discussion of investment risk in Chapter 2. And you can be sure that different aspects of risk and return will be mentioned throughout this book.

## Al-Location, Al-Location, Al-Location

Nearly everyone has heard of the phrase most synonymous with business success: "location, location, location." Building a successful business is very similar to building a successful portfolio. This classic wisdom applies to investment success as well, but expressed with a twist: "al-location, al-location, al-location." Location, or al-location in this case, can mean the difference between feast or famine. Moreover, where you locate can mean life or death of a business, and the same is true with investing. There are no shortcuts, and cutting corners can ultimately be an investor's downfall.

Before selecting a location, business owners do their homework; they do not rely on their own perceived superior instinct. They know that doing so will not get the job done. As an investor, you should approach your investing in the same manner. Prudent investors do not make the mistake of thinking that because their previous investment pick worked out, they are geniuses at picking new successful investments. Through experience you will know what constitutes a properly allocated portfolio and thus position yourself for long-term success.

Al-location is a factor whose true importance cannot be underestimated or underappreciated.

## Asset Allocation Analogy

To better help people understand the significant benefits of asset allocation, I often use a hockey analogy. The analogy goes something like this. Employing asset allocation is similar to a hockey player wearing protective equipment, such as a helmet, shoulder pads, knee pads, etc. If that hockey player were to take off his protective equipment, he could probably skate faster, cut easier, and pass the puck better. As a result, he would probably be a scoring machine. However, it doesn't take a rocket scientist to recognize that not wearing the proper protective equipment would be impractical and very unwise and foolish. One hit into the boards from his opponent and he could be out of the game for a very long time, if not forever. So why risk it?

It's the same with investing and asset allocation. An investor who does not wear his proper protective equipment may experience uncommonly superior returns in the short term, but will eventually take the same hit that a hockey player would and therefore could be badly hurt or out of the game completely. The investor may not take a hit right away, but it will happen at some point. The question is not if, but when.

## The Right Approach

Wealth building and wealth preservation have been important topics since the beginning of civilization. As long as people have been talking about taxes and empires, they have been talking about the intricacies of wealth management. Asset allocation itself is not a new strategy or the latest buzzword of investing. Investment management has undergone sweeping changes over the last several decades. It is alive, well, and offering very good advice today, as it has for thousands of years.

Building and maintaining a winning portfolio depends on how well a portfolio is designed, built, and managed. The primary determinant of how well a portfolio eventually performs over time is the asset allocation plan employed. When done the right way, you will experience reliable long-term performance over time. When done the wrong way, you will see little benefit aside from forming strong relationships with doctors needed to help you cope.

It is no secret that the majority of portfolio managers do not beat the return of the market each year. Furthermore, portfolio managers who do beat the market in any given year have a lower probability of beating the market in the following year. Approximately 80 percent of money managers do not surpass the return of the overall market in any given year. Quite surprising, isn't it? Why don't most money managers do better, especially given that they are paid to do so? Could the reason be poor market timing? How about careless stock picking? Or perhaps it is simply the result of bad luck? Research has shown none of those to be the correct answer. The principal reason the majority of portfolio managers do not beat the return of the overall market in any given year is because they failed to create, apply, and emphasize a sound asset allocation policy to the management of investment portfolios.

## Empirical Research Shows the Way

In 1986, a landmark study titled "Determinants of Portfolio Performance" published in the *Financial Analysts Journal* (July–August 1986, pp. 39–44), by Gary P. Brinson, L. Randolph Hood, and Gilbert L. Beebower concluded that asset allocation policy is by far the principal determinant of investment performance. Contrary to popular belief at the time, these researchers found that security selection and market timing determine only a small fraction of investment performance. See Figure 1-1.

• • • • • • • • • • • • • • • • • • • • • • • • • • • • • • •

*Asset Allocation:* The strategy of dividing an investor's wealth among the different asset classes and asset subclasses to achieve the highest expected total rate of return.

• • • • • • • • • • • • • • • • • • • • • • • • • • • • • • •

*Security Selection:* The strategy of determining which investments to buy or sell for a portfolio. Frequently referred to as stock picking.

• • • • • • • • • • • • • • • • • • • • • • • • • • • • • • •

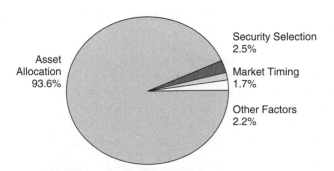

**Figure 1-1     Determinants of Investment Performance**

• • • • • • • • • • • • • • • • • • • • • • • • • • • • • •

*Market Timing*: The strategy of determining when to purchase or sell an investment.

• • • • • • • • • • • • • • • • • • • • • • • • • • • • • •

*Security:* An investable asset, excluding insurance policies, fixed annuities, and futures contracts, which can be purchased and sold.

• • • • • • • • • • • • • • • • • • • • • • • • • • • • • •

The aforementioned study was based on the quarterly investment results of 90 large pension funds over a 10-year period from 1974 to 1983. The goal of the study was to determine to what degree asset allocation policy, security selection, market timing, and, to a lesser extent, costs contributed to the investment performance of the pension funds under study.

Asset allocation policy was analyzed within the context of three primary asset classes: stocks, bonds, and cash. For example, one pension fund might have an asset mix of 65 percent stocks, 25 percent bonds, and 10 percent cash while another might have an asset mix of 50 percent stocks, 35 percent bonds, and 15 percent cash. Market timing was evaluated by analyzing the changes in asset class weightings over time. For instance, if a portfolio manager altered a pension fund's allocation to the three observed asset classes over a given time period, that was interpreted by the researchers as an attempt by the portfolio manager to profit from market timing. As you can see from Figure 1-1, asset allocation policy explained 93.6 percent of investment performance whereas security selection, market timing, and other factors (including costs) explained 2.5 percent, 1.7 percent, and 2.2 percent of investment performance, respectively.

In 1991, a follow-up study by Gary P. Brinson, Gilbert L. Beebower, and Brian D. Singer titled "Determinants of Portfolio Performance II: An Update" published in the *Financial Analysts Journal* (May–June 1991, pp. 40–48) was conducted using updated information. This study arrived at nearly the same conclusion as the previous study. As such, the subsequent study concluded that asset allocation policy is the primary factor explaining investment performance over time. The second study also found that security selection and market timing explained only a fraction of investment performance.

As you can see from Figure 1-2, asset allocation policy was found to explain 91.5 percent of investment performance while security selection, market timing, and other factors explained 4.6 percent, 1.8 percent, and 2.1 percent of investment performance, respectively.

In yet another significant research study, renowned practitioners Roger G. Ibbotson and Paul D. Kaplan in early 2000 concluded in their study titled "Does Asset Allocation Policy Explain 40, 90, or 100 Percent of Performance?" published in the *Financial Analysts Journal* (January–February 2000, pp. 26–33) that asset allocation policy explains about 90 percent of

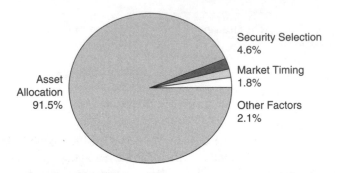

**Figure 1-2    Determinants of Investment Performance**

investment performance over time. A copy of this study can be obtained from the Ibbotson Associates company Web page at www.Ibbotson.com.

If security selection and market timing do not play a significant role in determining investment performance over time, a good question to ask is whether or not individual industries play a role. According to Eugene F. Fama and Kenneth R. French, they generally do not. In their research study titled "Industry Costs of Equity" published in the *Journal of Financial Economics* (1997), the researchers concluded that although specific industries can influence market prices, they do so only in a random and short-term way.

# Real-World Results

Let's step outside empirical research and consider real-world results. For an appropriate example, all you have to do is to look at the numerous financial magazines touting the best mutual funds to invest in for the upcoming year. Have you ever noticed how the majority of mutual funds that make those lists were not on the lists from the previous year or even the previous five years? Wait until next year and see which mutual funds make the best mutual funds lists. I bet you will discover very few that repeat. Regardless of whether or not these financial magazines are accurate with their picks, it clearly demonstrates how portfolio managers cannot beat the market consistently. If they could, then wouldn't there be more mutual funds repeating on the "best to invest in" lists? Focusing exclusively on security selection or market timing is similar to throwing a Hail Mary pass on every play in football (to use another sports analogy). Rather, investing is about gaining yardage successfully and consistently. Asset allocation is the strategy that will accomplish this task over time.

Contrary to whatever impression I may have given you, I am not opposed to security selection. Empirical evidence has concluded that it does explain a

| Returns on $10,000 invested annually in stocks and bonds 1984–2004 | |
| --- | --- |
| **Strategy** | **Average Annual Return** |
| Investing in previous year's best performing asset class | 9.55% |
| Investing in previous year's worst performing asset class | 8.12% |
| Investing evenly across asset classes | 10.65% |

**Figure 1-3   Asset Class Performance and Selection**

portion of investment performance over time. As a result, I believe security selection does have a place within the portfolio management process. However, you need to focus your time and resources on the strategy that will have a meaningful impact on your investment performance: namely, asset allocation. It is much more difficult to affect your investment performance via security selection or market timing than via asset allocation. You should emphasize asset allocation first, and then move to security selection or market timing if you so desire.

The chart in Figure 1-3 illustrates how the use of security selection by money managers and investors is a study in futility. As you can see, last year's winners are not this year's winners. The winning allocation was a portfolio mix of several asset classes. So much for asset allocation not promoting increased returns! Although last year's losers did not fare as well as this year's winners, the differential return was not significantly meaningful. Once you add in risk, the benefit of a properly allocated portfolio increases even more.

# Think You Have a Top Performer?

Consistent superior investment results require either superior information together with superior skill or simple plain old luck. Empirical research clearly shows that money managers typically do not deliver strong results year after year, even though this is a popular belief among investors. So why would anyone invest their money with a money manager who attempts to pick stocks or time the market? More than ever before, it appears that your best solution is to employ asset allocation. True, asset allocation is not sexy and can be considered boring at times, but no one can argue with its success and ability to deliver a performance edge.

Once you include money manager fees, the question of whether or not money managers beat their overall market target is even clearer. Paying management fees will decrease your return regardless of the return you receive. You will pay even if you lose money. Finding a low-cost investment vehicle that will implement your asset allocation plan is the best approach. In my judgment, index funds are the ideal investment for accomplishing this task, and I highly encourage you to investigate them and consider them for inclusion in your portfolio. Regardless of which investment vehicle you choose, your asset allocation is your primary decision. Your secondary and lower-priority decision is deciding which investment vehicle to use.

Finally, remember that all managed investment vehicles charge some degree of management fees. Hedge funds typically charge the highest fees, followed by mutual funds, and then index funds. Some index funds will charge as low as 0.19 percent annually. That translates into low cost, less siphoning from your investment return, and greater portfolio diversification.

## Old Rules for New Wealth

In simplistic terms, asset classes are the broadest investment categories you can invest in. These categories include equities, fixed-income, cash and equivalents, and alternative assets. Each of these "primary asset classes" can be further divided into "asset subclasses." These subclasses can include U.S. stocks and foreign stocks as well as corporate bonds and governmental bonds. Asset subclasses can then be divided even more, such as growth stocks and value stocks or long-term bonds and short-term bonds. By the way, *fixed-income* is simply another word for bonds. The two are used interchangeably in common practice, but sometimes it is not always appropriate to do so. Bonds are always considered fixed-income, but fixed-income is not always considered bonds.

Novice investors become successful investors by following the right approach. Asset allocation is that right approach. To become a successful investor you will need to study and learn about the various asset classes, their advantages and disadvantages, and how they can work together to create a truly optimal portfolio. Knowing the tax implications of each asset class and their return enhancement and risk reduction characteristics is highly beneficial. Determining and maintaining your asset allocation are the two most important investment decisions you can make in regard to your portfolio. As a result, I encourage you to learn as much as you can about asset allocation, asset classes, and multi-asset-class portfolios. Once you establish the optimal asset allocation for your unique situation, you will be well positioned for achieving your financial goals with a suitable level of risk.

## Asset Allocations Evolve over Time

Portfolios and the asset allocation comprising a portfolio will not remain static over time. At some point in the future your personal situation will change and in response so will your asset allocation. There are multiple factors that may change, and each plays a role in determining your optimal asset allocation. Some of these factors, called the *portfolio allocation inputs*, include your risk profile, your current and future financial position, and your investment time horizon. In addition to your personal situation changing, market factors that impact your portfolio will also change to some degree over time. These "market-centric" portfolio allocation inputs include expected total returns for your investments, the volatility risk of investments, and the trading flexibility of those investments you own and/or are targeting for investment purposes. Luckily, asset allocation promotes quick and easy changes to your portfolio. Thus you will not need to spend hour after hour researching what decisions should be made and then implementing them.

Please see Chapter 9 for an in-depth discussion of the portfolio allocation inputs and how they impact the process of determining your asset allocation. Chapter 9 also discusses the common methods and steps needed to properly determine your optimal asset allocation.

## Inside Winning Portfolios

Building a winning portfolio should be of utmost concern to investors looking to protect and grow their wealth. To build a winning portfolio, you will need to make some very important decisions. Each of these decisions is fully outlined and discussed in this book. A winning portfolio is a combination of a proper asset allocation, the right mix of investments to implement asset allocation, and the care and skill needed to make it happen. The right mix for each investor will differ and sometimes substantially. Some of the variables you will need to address when selecting the right mix includes tax structure, management fees, and trading costs. Given the vast options you have at your disposal, targeting diversified low-cost, tax-efficient investments is wise and ideally suited for your asset allocation plan. Index investments, which include both index mutual funds and exchange-traded funds, accomplish this with ease. These passively managed investments, which track specific markets, are on average about three times less expensive than actively managed funds. In addition, they provide the quickest and easiest way for you to gain immediate exposure to the asset classes you desire. Always remember to fully investigate your investment options. You will find lists of potential index investments after each chapter in Part Two, "Asset Class Alternatives."

Empirical research clearly shows that an investor's asset allocation is what drives portfolio performance over the long term. Let's put that macro viewpoint into a usable set of factors: a micro viewpoint. We will touch upon the following performance drivers throughout the book:

- The asset classes you will employ
- The percentage of your total portfolio that you will allocate to each asset class
- The parameters you set that trigger rebalancing—based on time or deviations
- The investment style you select—active management or index funds and their types
- The level of portfolio diversification
- The application of low correlations
- The tax status of your portfolio—tax-exempt or taxable
- The total tax bracket you are in

## Self-Assessment

Before embarking on your endeavor of properly allocating your assets and building a truly optimal portfolio, I highly encourage you to complete a self-assessment. Since asset allocation is a personalized process and will change over time as your situation changes, learn as much as you can about where you currently stand, what you are hoping to accomplish, and how best to bridge the gap. Different investors have different goals and objectives and varying financial circumstances and preferences. As a result, care, skill, and patience will be needed to reap the benefits of asset allocation.

## Key Benefits of Asset Allocation

So far you have already learned about the significant importance of asset allocation and the broad reasons supporting a properly allocated portfolio. But what are the more specific benefits of employing asset allocation? How will asset allocation most directly impact you and other individual investors? First and foremost, asset allocation will maximize the risk-adjusted return of anyone's portfolio—perhaps the most important reason for investing in the first place. In addition, asset allocation also minimizes portfolio volatility risk and provides for a sound investing discipline. This is in contrast to both security selection and market timing, two strategies that care little about reducing risk and instead aim for return only. This doesn't sound quite wise, given that risk and return are inescapably linked. Below are the key benefits of asset allocation, followed by detailed commentaries on each benefit.

- Minimizes retirement plan losses
- Promotes an optimal portfolio
- Eliminates what does not work
- Supports quick and easy reoptimization
- Maximizes portfolio risk-adjusted return
- Promotes simple portfolio design and construction
- Allows for easy contribution decisions
- Minimizes portfolio volatility
- Minimizes investor time and effort
- Promotes a more diversified portfolio
- Provides maximum avoidance of market weakness
- Delivers the highest impact value
- Reduces trading costs

## Minimizes Retirement Plan Losses

For most investors, retirement savings are their single largest personal accounts. Over time your portfolio may become quite large—and it should, since your future financial independence, security, and control depend on it. Many people receive employer retirement savings matching contributions through their 401(k) plan. Since asset allocation is built on the principles of the risk-and-return trade-off profile and diversification, in most cases asset allocation will limit the amount allocated to a single investment, namely that of your employer.

A good rule of thumb is to limit the allocation to your employer's stock and any other single investment to 10 percent of your entire portfolio. Any more than 10 percent should be reallocated to another investment or asset class. As a result of not overallocating to your employer's stock, your portfolio will not experience severe negative impacts from events involving your employer or any single investment. For real-world examples of how people were hurt by overallocating to the stock of their employer, simply think of the Enron, Tyco, and WorldCom debacles. Asset allocation will protect you from the impact of events such as these.

## Promotes an Optimal Portfolio

Each and every investor has a tolerance for risk as well as specific goals and needs. These goals are sometimes related to wealth accumulation,

wealth preservation, or both. Once you identify your risk profile and specific goals and needs, you are then able to design an optimal portfolio
that can best achieve them. More specifically, you want to earn suitable
portfolio performance over the long term. This is important because many
portfolios are designed with little regard for risk tolerance or goals and
needs. You should never design or have a portfolio that does not align
expected portfolio performance with what you want to accomplish. A
portfolio that aligns your goals and needs and risk profile with expected
portfolio performance provides you with your best chances for achieving
success. A sound plan will help you hit your target more often than will
throwing darts at a wall.

### Eliminates What Does Not Work

Asset allocation is the leading determinant of portfolio performance over
time. Why then would a portfolio be designed without employing asset allocation? Sometimes financial advisors employ excessive security selection
and market timing strategies in the hopes of earning excessive returns. Why
would you allow that with your investments? Security selection and market
timing have their place in managing your portfolio, but they must only be
employed within the context of a fully integrated asset allocation strategy.
In other words, make sure you allocate your portfolio properly and then
decide whether or not to employ the other two strategies. Asset allocation
takes much of the guesswork out of investing.

### Supports Quick and Easy Reoptimization

Of the three investment strategies—asset allocation, security selection, and
market timing—asset allocation allows for the quickest and easiest rebalancing. With security selection, you need to review each investment to determine
appropriateness and suitability and whether or not to buy or sell. This is
obviously a cumbersome endeavor. Market timing is even more cumbersome
since not only must an investor evaluate an investment's prospects but the
investor must also keep a constant eye on when to buy or sell.

On the other hand, asset allocation uses strict guidelines for making
modifications. These guidelines are generally expressed as floors and ceilings. *Floors* and *ceilings* are target allocation ranges in which allocations are
permitted to move before changes need to be made. If allocations are within
the target allocation ranges, then rebalancing is not necessary. However,
once allocations move outside the target ranges, rebalancing is triggered. In
simplistic terms, rebalancing involves selling overallocated investments and
buying underallocated investments.

## Maximizes Portfolio Risk-Adjusted Return

The objective of asset allocation is to provide the highest return for your risk profile: tolerance for risk, capacity for risk, and need for risk. As a result, not only does asset allocation maximize return but it also minimizes risk. In doing so, asset allocation is said to provide the highest possible risk-adjusted return.

Asset allocation is founded on two investment theories: modern portfolio theory (MPT) and efficient market hypothesis (EMH). Modern portfolio theory says that when an investor is faced with two investments with identical expected returns, but different levels of risk, he or she should select the investment that has the lower risk. Therefore, a rational investor will select the investment with the higher return when faced with two investments that have different expected returns but identical levels of risk. This is the premise of the risk-averse investor. The efficient market hypothesis, a term coined by Eugene F. Fama, says that security prices are fair and reasonable because they fully reflect all available public and nonpublic information that might impact them. As a result, security selection and market timing will fail over the long term since every investor has the same information with no investor thus gaining an edge over another. By combining investments with different returns and risk levels, you will build a portfolio that provides the maximum risk-adjusted return.

## Promotes Simple Portfolio Design and Construction

In comparison to market timing and security selection, asset allocation facilitates a quick and easy approach to building your optimal portfolio. Index funds and exchange-traded funds make the task even quicker and easier, given their inherent advantages and benefits of integrating with asset allocation.

When building a portfolio with asset allocation, you should select appropriate asset classes based on your goals and needs, risk profile, and time horizon. Given the breadth and depth of asset classes, it is possible to select a minimal number of asset classes and fully accomplish your goal of building an optimal portfolio. On the other hand, security selection necessitates evaluating numerous investments for consideration in a portfolio whereas market timing must evaluate both suitability and when to buy or sell. Determining precise times can be a challenge and thus make the design and construction of your portfolio a burden. Asset allocation is the ultimate solution when it comes to building a portfolio quickly and easily.

## Allows for Easy Contribution Decisions

With security selection and market timing, an evaluation of investments must be made to determine whether or not to invest in a particular asset. With asset allocation, all new contributions should be allocated to those asset classes that have lower than optimal allocations. No fancy computer programs or mathematical calculations are needed when making contributions within the context of an asset allocation strategy. In reality, you can determine by quick mathematics which allocation is below the optimal allocation and therefore identify where to make the contribution. A peripheral benefit to this approach is that you are rebalancing to a certain level and ensuring your portfolio remains optimal. That, of course, is important to ensure that your portfolio performance is aligned to achieve your goals and objectives.

## Minimizes Portfolio Volatility

By allocating to multiple asset classes that do not move in perfect lockstep with each other, your portfolio will be shielded from excessive and unacceptable portfolio volatility. At times, one asset class or investment will perform well while at other times another asset class or investment will perform well. If you were to have only a portfolio of fixed-income securities, then you would experience weakness in your total portfolio rather than experiencing a more balanced approach with both fixed-income and equities.

## Minimizes Investor Time and Effort

This key benefit is more or less common sense. Asset allocation does not keep you glued to the market on a daily basis, whereas market timing and, to a lesser degree, security selection, do. As long as your financial position, goals, objectives, and needs do not change, your primary responsibility will be to review and evaluate your present allocation mix against your previously established optimal asset mix. Until allocations move outside of the allocation range, no rebalancing action is triggered.

On the other hand, high maintenance is a defining characteristic of market timing. One cannot simply employ market timing and a hands-off approach at the same time. Security selection, although clearly not as demanding of your time as market timing, still requires more time and attention than does asset allocation. Finally, since asset allocation provides the greatest risk-adjusted return, the value for employing asset allocation is magnified, given the minimal time and effort required.

## Promotes a More Diversified Portfolio

Along with exchange-traded funds and index funds, asset allocation promotes a more diversified portfolio. But how important is diversification? *Diversification* is a strategy designed to reduce total risk by combining a large number of securities within a particular asset class that exhibit similar risk-and-return trade-off profiles. Diversification is one of the ten cornerstone principles of asset allocation.

Diversifying your portfolio is absolutely critical to control and minimize the risk in your portfolio. Diversification allows you to minimize the impact from a negative investment-specific event, such as a corporate CFO cooking the books. Do you recall the WorldCom debacle? The big question is how can you build a properly diversified portfolio? You basically have two options. First, you can purchase a significant number of securities with similar risk-and-return trade-off profiles. This process can be challenging and burdensome. Or you can go the quick, easy, and highly effective route and purchase exchange-traded funds. Given their defining characteristic, exchange-traded funds are the most diversified investments in the marketplace for any particular asset class, and since 1999 have grown by leaps and bounds. Consequently, you have ample exchange-traded funds to choose from.

## Provides Maximum Avoidance of Market Weakness

Over the history of the stock market, investors have experienced some market crashes and numerous periods of prolonged market weakness. At times, one asset class will perform well whereas at other times another asset class will perform well. Asset allocation has been shown to not only control risk but also to minimize the impact from portfolio crashes. Protecting portfolio value is one of the leading benefits of employing asset allocation.

> EXAMPLE: The Jones's portfolio had 50 percent in equities, 30 percent in fixed-income, 10 percent in alternative assets, and 10 percent in cash and equivalents. Within 10 months after portfolio construction, the equity market experienced a sharp 15 percent decline in value. Given the allocation in the Jones's portfolio, the total value of the portfolio declined by only 7½ percent. This decline was most likely offset by gains in the other asset classes, particularly fixed-income.

By combining asset classes with different correlations, your portfolio will be able to ride out market weakness and the impact of market crashes.

## Delivers the Highest Impact Value

Impact value can be defined as the value an investor will receive from employing a specific investment strategy: benefit divided by the costs (time and money) needed to employ that strategy. Minimizing costs without addressing rewards provides only minimal value. Specifically, asset allocation not only maximizes the risk-adjusted return of your portfolio but also provides for the lowest costs to employ that strategy. Security selection and market timing require somewhat greater costs while delivering only marginal results. In consequence, asset allocation provides the greatest impact value, thus deserving a place within your portfolio.

## Reduces Trading Costs

Asset allocation calls for rebalancing when allocations are either above allocation range ceilings or below allocation range floors. As a result of this disciplined approach, trades may need to be made less frequently than with security selection and market timing. Furthermore, asset allocation tends to emphasize fewer numbers of holdings than both security selection and market timing. Thus, both the frequency and amount of rebalancing tend to be much lower than with the other investment strategies.

Since market timing and security selection emphasize more trading, these two investment strategies tend to promote greater capital gains tax consequences than does asset allocation. In addition, most capital gains tax consequences from market timing are short-term capital gains, which are typically taxed at a higher rate than are long-term capital gains. Security selection and asset allocation provide for relatively equal capital gains tax consequences.

In the next chapter, you will learn about the basics of investment risk and return.

# Understanding Investment Risk and Return

No matter how skillful the trading scheme, over the long haul, abnormal returns are sustained only through abnormal exposure to risk.

*—ALAN GREENSPAN,*
*FORMER FEDERAL RESERVE CHAIRMAN*

No one particularly likes risk. Furthermore, no one particularly likes risk when risk becomes reality and misfortune results. Avoiding risk is therefore highly ideal. However, doing so is not entirely feasible in the world of investing, since there is a clear and profound relationship between risk and return. Risk is an inherent part of any investment undertaking, so it is essential that investors understand this inescapable trade-off. Of course, there is the potential for strong returns, but investors can get blindsided by the magnitude of risk if they aren't careful.

Unfortunately, we hear the very opposite practically every day. In many areas of our lives, we are told that reward can be earned with little to no risk. Since you are reading this book, I am confident that you understand that reward without risk does not exist in the investment marketplace. And don't let anyone tell you otherwise. Abnormally high returns are not uncommon, but they are neither predictable nor consistent over time. Consequently, if you desire a return that outpaces both inflation and taxes, then you must be prepared to assume some level of risk. You get what you pay for and earn what you invest in. No one gets something for nothing.

Two of the most important concepts an investor should learn and fully understand are *investment return* and *investment risk*. These two concepts and how they work together are the foundations of asset allocation and its application to building an optimal portfolio. Depending on your objectives and constraints, you may invest in assets that exhibit low risk and therefore the potential for low, but stable returns or you may invest in assets that exhibit high risk and therefore the potential for high, but volatile returns. In basic asset allocation theory, the higher the potential risk you take, the higher the potential return you can earn. Rational investors will not assume a higher level of risk if they don't have to.

The million-dollar question is how to enhance your returns and still avoid risk. Although risk cannot be entirely eliminated from a portfolio, it can be controlled and managed with a proper asset allocation policy. A portfolio that is optimally designed, built, and managed will exhibit a higher risk-adjusted return than a portfolio that does not subscribe to proper asset allocation, regardless of its high return investments. This is exemplified by Modern Portfolio Theory. After learning the risk-and-reward profiles of each asset class, you will then be able to build your own portfolio with an acceptable level of risk and expected return. The next section of this chapter will discuss investment return followed by an in-depth discussion of investment risk. The final section will discuss the important relationship between investment risk and investment return.

## Understanding Investment Return

Investment return is of primary importance. Otherwise, why would you invest? Without appropriate compensation in the form of returns, people would not invest their hard-earned money. Earning the highest return for the least amount of risk assumed is at the core of asset allocation. Return can come in many different ways. Although we will be discussing quantitative measures of return, do not forget that return often has qualitative rewards. Qualitative rewards include comfort, peace of mind, security, simplicity, and a feeling of control over one's life.

It is vitally important that you consider the return you wish to receive and what risk you must assume to obtain that return. Moreover, investing more money in a higher return asset class does not mean your return will be any higher than if you had invested less in that same asset class. It is not the individual investments comprising your portfolio that are important; rather, it is the portfolio as a whole that is most important. For this reason, it is wise to build a portfolio of multiple asset classes rather than allocating to only the current high return potential asset class. Generally speaking, a higher probability of return also means a higher probability of losing some or all of an investment. Some people are willing to assume that risk, whereas others are not. This is what makes asset allocation and portfolio construction so unique from person to person.

• • • • • • • • • • • • • • • • • • • • • • • • • • • • • • • •

*Investment Return:* The profit or loss an investor receives for making an investment. Expressed in both dollar and percentage terms.

• • • • • • • • • • • • • • • • • • • • • • • • • • • • • • • •

The profit or loss from an investment is comprised of both, appreciation or depreciation in market value over the holding period plus dividends or interest received during the same holding period. Summing the two profit or loss components and dividing by the market value of the investment at the beginning of the period will give what is referred to as *total return.* This measure takes into account both the change in price of the security and any cash flow received during the holding period. It is commonplace in the investment field to measure return using the total return calculation. An example of calculating total return is as follows:

> EXAMPLE: The Deneanu Foundation purchased 1,000 shares of Deere & Co. at $40 a share. One year later the Jones Foundation sold the investment for $44 a share. During the one-year period, Deere & Co. paid a $1 per share dividend. The total return of the investment, not including transaction costs, is 12.5 percent ($4 appreciation plus $1 dividend divided by $40 cost). Thus, to calculate total return, sum the appreciation (ending value less the beginning value) and all interest and dividends received during the period and divide by the beginning value.

The concept of return can be divided into two distinctions: actual return and expected return. *Actual return* is the return you have realized or one that has occurred in a past holding period. Conversely, *expected return* is an estimate of what you will earn, both appreciation and income (dividends and interest), in a future holding period. Both actual and expected returns are commonly expressed as annualized percentages. The process of forecasting expected returns is especially difficult. However, the following basic steps will provide you with a cursory understanding:

- Forecast all possible material outcomes that may occur.
- Assign probabilities of occurrence to each outcome.
- Forecast the return for each specific material outcome.
- Multiply the probabilities with their related forecasted return.
- Add the results for each possible outcome.

EXAMPLE: An analyst estimates that the Smith Company has a 50 percent probability of returning 12 percent, a 25 percent probability of returning 5 percent, a 15 percent probability of returning 0 percent, and a 10 percent probability of returning –5 percent. Thus, the estimated return is:

$$(.50 \times .12) + (.25 \times .05) + (.15 \times 0) + [.10 \times (-.05)] = 6.75 \text{ percent}$$

Potential outcomes are usually based on estimates of how well the economy will perform in the future holding period. The resulting return is simply an estimate given each economic scenario.

## Understanding Investment Risk

Investment risk can be defined in many different ways, and each investor views risk differently. Some investors define risk as losing money, while others define risk as unfamiliar investments. Still others define risk as contrarian risk, or how risk investors feel when they are not "following the crowd." If you were to toss out all of the subjective definitions, *risk* is defined more objectively as uncertainty, or the uncertainty that actual returns will equal expected returns. Pension funds and insurance companies view risk as the uncertainty they can meet future benefit obligations whereas mutual funds view risk as underperformance compared to peer mutual funds and/or an industry benchmark, such as the S&P 500. As for individual investors, they tend to view risk as losing money in their portfolios, whether that loss is temporary or permanent. This may not be the best method for viewing risk, but it is the most understood and most commonly applied by individual investors.

In my judgment, viewing risk as the uncertainty of meeting future funding obligations is the most sensible. These funding obligations can be paying for college expenses, making property tax payments, starting a new business, or simply supplementing social security to pay for expenses in the golden years. No person wants to lose his or her hard-earned money, run out of it early, or even outlive it long into retirement.

Overall, most investment experts define risk quite rigidly as the volatility of returns over a specific time period. Most risk measurements are accomplished using monthly price movements for individual securities, whether those movements are up or down. The greater the monthly movement, regardless of direction, the larger the volatility measure and therefore the greater the risk. Volatility also impacts total performance. Portfolios with more volatility will exhibit lower long-term compounded growth rates of return. Thus, it is essential to minimize volatility in your portfolio for maximum appreciation over time.

Risk management and proper asset allocation reduce both the frequency and the amount of portfolio losses. Since you rely on estimates of future returns to design your optimal portfolio, it is critically important that actual returns come close to matching expected returns. Investments with more predictable returns are considered lower risk. Conversely, investments with less predictable returns are considered higher risk.

• • • • • • • • • • • • • • • • • • • • • • • • • • • • • • •

*Risk:* In one word, risk can be called *uncertainty.* More specifically, the uncertainty that actual returns will match expected returns.

• • • • • • • • • • • • • • • • • • • • • • • • • • • • • • •

## Asset Classes and Risk

Different asset classes possess different types and amounts of risk and therefore different expected returns. Each type of risk is derived from one or more sources of risk. Regardless of the type and source of investment risk, asset allocation will allow you to control and manage your risk exposure to your best advantage. Asset allocation is the key to total risk reduction.

As previously mentioned, however, it is simply not enough to focus on the merits of one particular investment, since it is how each investment moves in relation to the other investments that truly matters. Regardless of the risk-and-return potential for each asset, keep in mind that understanding their fundamentals and how they impact a portfolio is most important.

## Sources of Investment Risk

There are two primary sources of risk. The first is called *systematic risk,* or risk attributed to relatively uncontrollable external factors. The second is called *unsystematic risk,* or risk attributed directly to the underlying investment.

### Systematic Risk

Systematic risk results from conditions, events, and trends occurring outside the scope of the investment. At any one point, different degrees of risk are occurring. These risks will cause the demand for a particular investment to rise or fall, thus impacting actual returns. The four principal types of systematic risk include the following:

- *Exchange Rate Risk*: The risk that an investment's value will be impacted by changes in the foreign currency market. For example, if you own a foreign asset, then changes in the value of that foreign currency relative to the U.S. dollar will impact your return. If the U.S. dollar increases in value, then your return declines since it will take more foreign currency to buy one U.S. dollar. For the opposite reason, a declining U.S. dollar will increase your return.
- *Interest Rate Risk*: The risk attributed to the loss in market value due to an increase in the general level of interest rates. Why do market values decline when interest rates rise? Primarily because as interest rates rise, the availability of more attractive investments with higher yields also increases. For example, if you owned a bond yielding 5 percent and interest rates increased by 1 percent to 6 percent, then demand for higher yielding bonds would increase, lowering the yield on your bond, thus a decrease in return.
- *Market Risk*: The risk attributed to the loss in market value due to the declining movement of the entire market portfolio. Here no particular investment is singled out as the entire market takes a hit. When the market sells off hard, most investments sell off as well. If they didn't, then how could the market fall?
- *Purchasing Power Risk*: The risk attributed to inflation and how it erodes the real value of an investment over time. Inflation increases prices to varying degrees. This means $100 today will buy less in one year. Your investment dollars are impacted the same way.

## Unsystematic Risk

Unlike systematic risk, unsystematic risk is not attributed to external factors. This source of risk is unique to an investment, such as how much debt a company possesses, what actions a company's management takes, and what industry it operates in. The principal types of unsystematic risk include the following:

- *Business Risk*: The risk attributed to a company's operations, particularly those involving sales and income. Persistent declining sales spell trouble and increase an investment's risk. Rising sales are viewed favorably and translate into higher returns.
- *Financial Risk*: The risk attributed to a company's financial stability and structure, namely the company's use of debt to leverage earnings. Com-

panies with more debt have higher debt interest payments, including the repayment of principle. In good times, companies typically can make these payments easily. However, in bad times, their ability is hampered. As a result, companies with more debt are considered riskier.

- *Industry Risk*: The risk attributed to a group of companies within a particular industry. Investments tend to rise and fall based on what their peers are doing. A big move in price to the upside will bode well for other stocks in that industry group.
- *Liquidity Risk*: The risk that an investment cannot be purchased or sold at a price at or near market prices. The more liquid a market, the more buyers and sellers and thus the easier it is to buy or sell at current market prices. Illiquidity can cause you to sell at a much lower price than expected.
- *Call Risk*: The risk attributed to an event where an investment may be called prior to maturity. This may leave the investor unable to reinvest the proceeds at the same or a higher rate of return. This risk is associated with bonds and preferred stock.
- *Regulation Risk*: The risk that new laws and regulations will negatively impact the market value of an investment. For example, a state government may pass a law requiring manufacturers to add new and costly pollution control systems in their factories. Complying with this law will take money, potentially reducing the financial position of a company.

Systematic risk plus unsystematic risk equals total risk. Since the goal of asset allocation is to create a well-diversified portfolio, unsystematic risk is considered unimportant because with proper diversification it would not be a problem. In other words, an optimal portfolio should only possess systematic risk, or risk resulting from market and other uncontrollable external factors.

# Measuring Investment Risk

Since different investments have both different types of risk and different degrees of risk, it is essential to quantify risk in order to make comparisons across the broad range of asset classes. As mentioned earlier, risk can be defined as the uncertainty that actual returns will match expected returns. Intuitively one can see that the greater the difference between actual and expected returns, the less predictable and the more uncertain that investment is considered to be. This translates into greater risk.

Using historical return data, we are able to define risk more accurately. Historical volatility data can be obtained using numerous intervals of time: days, weeks, month, and years. Monthly volatility is generally used in practice. In simple analysis, averaging the degrees of difference between actual and expected returns for a given investment gives us the statistical measure called *standard deviation*. A higher standard deviation means higher risk. Historically, small-cap stocks have the highest average standard deviation at about 20 percent while the average standard deviation for long-term stocks over the same period is about 15 percent. Most classes of bonds historically exhibit standard deviations of less than 1 percent.

*Note:* Standard deviations for investments or asset classes are not static. They will change over time. Some asset classes will change more frequently and to a greater degree than other asset classes. Historically, small-cap stocks have exhibited the greatest amount of variability with regard to standard deviation. Large-cap stocks follow right behind.

Volatility has been shown to rise during periods of falling prices and remain moderate during periods of advancing prices. Even with changes to asset class volatility in the short term, the range of asset class volatility has remained relatively stable over the long term. That is good for investment planning.

• • • • • • • • • • • • • • • • • • • • • • • • • • • • • • •

*Standard Deviation:* A statistical measure of the degree to which actual returns are spread around the mean actual return. Expressed as a percentage, standard deviation is considered the best measure of risk.

• • • • • • • • • • • • • • • • • • • • • • • • • • • • • • •

Since actual returns are impacted by both systematic and unsystematic risks, standard deviation is a measure of total risk. As a result, standard deviation gives an investor a way to evaluate both the risk-and-return element of an individual investment. Although standard deviation is one of the best measures of risk, it is not without issues. Depending on the holding periods selected for comparison, standard deviation may vary from analysis to analysis. Due to many factors, it is best to use a standard deviation that is derived from actual returns from the last 10 to 20 years. Using returns older than 20 years may incorporate risks in the investment which are no longer present or were not present over 20 years ago. For example, 30 years ago tobacco companies were not inundated with class-action lawsuits regarding the health concerns of smoking. Today these class-action lawsuits can have a significant impact on their stock prices. Consequently, it is more appropriate to use data collected from recent periods to calculate standard deviation.

• • • • • • • • • • • • • • • • • • • • • • • • • • • • • • •

*Beta:* A measure of risk. The degree of security price volatility in relation to the overall market. Expressed as an absolute number rather than as a percentage.

• • • • • • • • • • • • • • • • • • • • • • • • • • • • • • •

Another common measure of risk is called *beta*. This measure is easier to understand, calculate, and apply than standard deviation. However, it too has drawbacks. The most significant drawback is not being representative of total risk. Beta is derived from the volatility of a given investment relative to the overall market. Thus, beta only measures systematic, or market risk, and not unsystematic, or investment-specific risk. Remember, however, that a properly built portfolio will have minimal unsystematic risk.

Beta is expressed in absolute rather than percentage terms. A beta of above 1.0 is considered more volatile than the market, whereas a beta of less than 1.0 is considered less volatile than the overall market. Yes, you guessed it; betas of 1.0 move in sync with the overall market. Thus, if an investment has a beta of 1.5, that investment will be 50 percent more volatile than the overall market whereas an investment with a beta of 0.75 will be 25 percent less volatile than the overall market.

> EXAMPLE: Stock A has a beta of 1.2. Thus, if the S&P 500 were expected to rise by 5 percent during the holding period, then Stock A is expected to rise by 6 percent (5 percent multiplied by 1.2). Conversely, if the S&P 500 were expected to fall by 5 percent during the holding period, then Stock A is expected to fall by 6 percent.

As you can see from the above example, when the market is rising, higher beta investments generally earn higher returns than the overall market. Conversely, when the market is declining, these same investments generally have lower returns than the overall market. In practice, investors desiring market rates of return can generally obtain them by investing in securities with betas of 1.0 or relatively close. Moreover, investors desiring to be more aggressive can potentially obtain higher returns by investing in securities with betas higher than 1.0. Of course, securities with betas above 1.0 have more inherent risk.

## Risk-Free Treasuries Myth

United States Treasury bills, or T-bills for short, have the lowest risk and therefore the lowest return of any investment in the United States. Having the lowest level of risk is a good thing, or perhaps it is not. One of the leading misconceptions in the marketplace is that these very securities are entirely risk-free. Risk-free from what is the question. Yes, it is true that Treasuries are considered default-free given the government's guarantee. Therefore, investors do not have to worry about losing their money. However, T-bills provide for a return, albeit positive, that is so low that often it does not even outpace the siphoning effects of both inflation and taxes. For example, the real return (return less inflation) after taxes on T-bills during the period

2001–2004 was actually below the rate of inflation. This means that investors holding T-bills during this time saw their purchasing power decline. Remember, to earn a return in excess of inflation and taxes, you must assume some level of risk.

Fortunately, the Federal Reserve has issued relatively newer types of Treasury securities that are protected against inflation risk. These securities are Treasury Inflation Protected Securities (TIPS) and I-Bonds. To combat inflation, the maturity values of these Treasuries increase with the rate of inflation. In consequence, when the investment reaches maturity, the investor will receive a slightly greater amount due to inflation. Purchasing power is thus restored.

## Ten Rules of Risk Reduction

Risk, and the endeavor to reduce risk, is as old as the financial markets themselves. Regardless of the new technology, the new hot products, or the new financial models, successful investing is all about maximizing the inescapable trade-off between risk and return. The following is a list of 10 rules that can help you reduce the level of risk in your portfolio.

1. *Knowing Your Level of Portfolio:* risk will enable you to make better and more informed decisions.
2. *Build a Multi-Asset-Class Portfolio:* Holding multiple asset classes will smooth the risk volatility you would otherwise experience from holding only one asset class.
3. *Target Low Correlations:* Low correlations further smooth out risk volatility since lower correlations mean the two asset classes will not always move in tandem with each other.
4. *Add Fundamentally Different Asset Classes:* Asset classes that are fundamentally different will exhibit enhanced return and risk reduction potential. Hold a combination of these asset classes.
5. *Diversify Each Asset Class:* Diversification is not the same as asset allocation. Diversify each asset class to reduce unsystematic risk, or investment-specific risk unique to single investments.
6. *Reoptimize Your Portfolio:* Reoptimization involves rebalancing your allocation mix to optimal targets, reallocating contributions to under-allocated asset classes, and reallocating assets for maximum tax and income efficiency.
7. *Use Common Sense:* When selecting the suitable level of risk for your portfolio, it is more important to be approximately correct than to be precisely wrong.

8. *Hedge Risk:* Although not for all investors, hedging risk with options, swaps, futures, and position-neutralizing short sales can protect against severe market declines.
9. *Exercise Discipline:* Employing a steadfast approach to enhancing your risk-adjusted return will outperform a constantly changing approach.
10. *Consider Assistance:* Risk is best managed by experienced people, not financial models. Professional help may provide you with the resources you need.

## Risk-and-Return Relationship

In principle, investors who take greater risk should be compensated with greater return. Depending on your risk profile, the more risk you assume, the higher your expected return. To better understand this relationship between risk and expected return, a model called the *efficient frontier* was developed. The efficient frontier plots different investments on an upward-sloping curved line according to their risk-and-return trade-off profile.

• • • • • • • • • • • • • • • • • • • • • • • • • • • • • •

*Efficient Frontier:* All possible optimal portfolio combinations where the expected total rate of return is maximized given the specific level of risk assumed. Usually illustrated as a curved line.

• • • • • • • • • • • • • • • • • • • • • • • • • • • • • •

As you can see from Figure 2-1, by moving up the efficient frontier, investments present the potential for greater return, but also for greater risk. Nevertheless, each point on the efficient frontier exhibits the highest expected total rate of return for the level of risk present.

Your objective is to select investments somewhere along the efficient frontier within the context of your objectives and constraints. Some investors will place their investments toward the top of the slope whereas others with lower risk tolerances will place their investments on a lower part of the slope. An investor approaching retirement, for example, will begin moving down the slope while a person approaching peak earning years may move up the slope as his or her tolerance for risk becomes greater.

Regardless of whether your portfolio is comprised of 50 percent equities and 50 percent fixed-income or 40 percent equities, 40 percent fixed-income, and 20 percent cash and equivalents, as long as each portfolio combination exhibits the highest expected total rate of return it will be plotted somewhere along the efficient frontier. Portfolios that do not exhibit the highest expected total rates of return will be plotted below the slope of the efficient frontier.

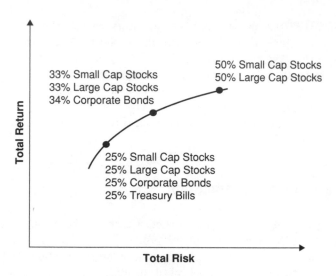

**Figure 2-1    Hypothetical Efficient Frontier**

Understanding the relationship between risk and return is critical as it underlies the process of allocating assets. Without a true understanding of this relationship, you may design a portfolio with either greater risk than desired or earn lower actual returns from less risky assets. As we will see in the next few chapters, the process of asset allocation involves estimating expected returns for each asset class and then determining, within the context of your objectives and constraints, what percentage of the portfolio should be allocated to each asset class.

## Risk-and-Return Trade-off

Given the direct relationship between risk and return, investors are able to measure this relationship and use that measurement to build a portfolio with the appropriate risk-and-return trade-off profile. By using what is called the *Sharpe Ratio*, or simply dividing the excess expected return of an asset class by its standard deviation (level of risk), we are able to ascertain the amount of excess expected return per unit of risk for an asset class. Doing so helps us to compare, contrast, and select asset classes with dissimilar excess expected returns and risk levels. Excess expected return is the expected return minus the risk-free rate, or the rate one can earn from investing in U.S. Treasury bills.

EXAMPLE: Suppose we have two asset classes, A and B. Asset class A has a standard deviation of 6 percent and an excess expected return of 8 percent over the proposed holding period. By dividing the excess expected return of 8 percent by the standard deviation of 6 percent, we find that asset class A has a risk-and-return trade-off profile of 1.33. Asset class B has a standard deviation of 4 percent and an excess expected return of 6 percent. This translates into a risk-and-return trade-off profile of 1.5. As you can see, although asset class A has the higher expected return, it clearly does not provide the highest level of expected return per unit of risk, as does asset class B.

• • • • • • • • • • • • • • • • • • • • • • • • • • • • • • • •

*Sharpe Ratio:* A method developed by William F. Sharpe to measure the risk-adjusted return of an investment or portfolio. This method calculates the amount of excess return per unit of risk.

• • • • • • • • • • • • • • • • • • • • • • • • • • • • • • •

In the next chapter, you will learn about all of the essentials of asset allocation and hopefully gain a better understanding of how to make it work for you.

3

# Essentials of
# Asset Allocation

As mentioned in Chapter 1, asset allocation is founded on two celebrated and highly influential investment theories. These two are the modern portfolio theory (MPT) and the efficient market hypothesis (EMH), which is essentially a refinement of MPT.

The modern portfolio theory says that investors and portfolio managers should not evaluate each investment on a stand-alone basis. Rather, each investment should be evaluated based on its ability to enhance the overall risk-and-return profile of a portfolio. When faced with two investments with identical expected returns but different levels of risk, investors should select the investment that has the lower risk according to the modern portfolio theory. Or, a rational investor will select the investment with the higher return when faced with two investments that have different expected returns but identical levels of risk.

Figure 3-1 illustrates the MPT. When faced with investments A and B, a rational investor will select investment B over investment A because the total return of investment B is higher, with both having the same level of risk. Moreover, when faced with investments B and C, a rational investor will select investment C over investment B because the total risk of investment C is lower, with both having the same total return. Pretty simple stuff, but it was revolutionary when first put forth.

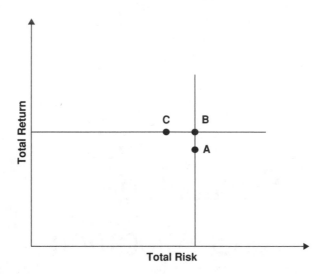

**Figure 3-1    Investment Alternatives and Rational Decisions**

Lastly, modern portfolio theory introduces the concept of correlation and stresses how it enhances the risk-and-return profile of a portfolio. The Employee Retirement Income Security Act of 1974, which governs the management of pension funds, emphasizes this point, thus essentially endorsing MPT. Harry M. Markowitz, who was awarded the Nobel Prize in Economics in 1990, is considered the "father of modern portfolio theory" for this work.

The *efficient market hypothesis*, a term coined by Eugene F. Fama, says that security prices are fair and reasonable because they fully reflect all available public and nonpublic information that might impact them. As a result, security selection and market timing will fail over the long term since every investor has the same information with no investor thus gaining an edge over another.

The efficient market hypothesis concludes therefore that the amount of risk that investors take determines their investment performance over time. Contrary to misconception, the EMH concludes that investors can beat the market. Over any holding period there will be some investors who will beat the market, but most will not. The number of investors who beat the market will be no greater than expected by standard mathematical probability. Statistical outliers are common given the law of large numbers.

For the sake of argument, let's say the market is not completely efficient and therefore sizeable opportunities do exist with which to beat the market. This assumption raises an important question. Do individual investors have the means and ability to take advantage of these opportunities? Unfortunately, very few do. Given our increasingly competitive investment environment and accelerating developments in information technology, undervalued securities exist for very short periods. With the vast number of highly skilled investment professionals and sophisticated financial trading programs, these undervalued securities disappear very quickly. The question then is what does this mean in practice to you and me? The answer is the creation of exceedingly efficient financial markets where investors cannot earn consistently superior investment returns, and where risk and return are inescapably and invariably linked.

## Theory Meets Practice

As mentioned in the previous chapter, asset allocation is the principal determinant of investment performance over time. A proper asset allocation policy will not only achieve your specific financial goals but will also protect your portfolio from serious market corrections. The primary aim of asset allocation is to maximize your portfolio's expected total rate of return for the level of risk that you have the tolerance, capacity, and need to assume. Depending on the scenario, with the proper asset allocation policy, you may even increase your investment return without increasing risk.

In addition to maximizing the expected return for the level of risk you assume, asset allocation also reduces portfolio volatility. More asset classes and asset subclasses equate to less portfolio volatility. Since asset classes perform differently at different times, during any one period, one asset class may perform well, while another may not. Allocating to multiple asset classes is thus advisable.

As with most everything, one size does not fit all with asset allocation either. Depending on your unique circumstances and preferences, you may customize your portfolio by allocating more or less to each asset class. Consequently, if you desire more return and have the willingness, capacity, and need to assume more risk, you can allocate more to higher-risk asset classes. Conversely, assuming less risk can be accomplished by allocating more of your assets to lower-risk asset classes.

## The Personalized Program

How to determine your asset allocation—which asset classes you invest in and in what percentage—is largely based on your investment objectives and constraints. These investor-centric inputs, together with investment-centric inputs, provide for a method to allocate your assets. Chapter 9 discusses in greater detail each input for the portfolio allocation methods.

Investment objectives are your return aspiration, such as protecting capital or receiving current income, and your risk profile. Investment constraints, on the other hand, are parameters and limitations that must be adhered to when building and managing your portfolio.

In practice, portfolio managers focus on two objectives: return aspiration and risk tolerance. Likewise, portfolio managers focus on five constraints: time horizon, liquidity needs, tax considerations, legal and regulatory considerations, and unique circumstances and preferences. A brief definition of each is offered below.

## Investment Objectives

*Return Aspiration:* The financial reward sought by an investor for investing and deferring current consumption.

*Risk Profile:* The degree of risk an investor can assume. This profile is based on an investor's willingness to assume risk, capacity to assume risk, and need to assume risk.

## Investment Constraints

*Time Horizon:* The length of time an investor plans to invest. Time horizon is also referred to as time period or holding period.

*Liquidity Needs:* The degree to which an investor requires cash and its equivalents to support everyday activities and special purchases.

*Tax Considerations:* The attention that is given to realizing, deferring, or avoiding taxes.

*Legal and Regulatory Considerations*: Laws and regulations that an investor and portfolio manager are obligated to follow.

*Unique Circumstances and Preferences*: This constraint essentially incorporates anything that cannot be categorized in one of the other four constraints. An example is unusual preferences of the investor that impair or challenge the portfolio management process in some way.

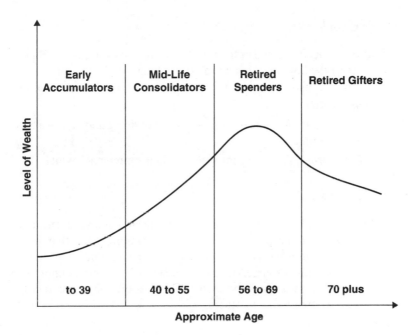

**Figure 3-2   Life Cycle Phases**

Your objectives and constraints will change over time. As a result, each stage in your life will have a significant impact on the investment process. There are three primary life-cycle phases, as seen in Figure 3-2.

Although not always the case, people in each life-cycle phase tend to share similar needs and goals. As you can see from Figure 3-2, the primary factor underlying each life-cycle phase is wealth. As people accumulate more wealth over time, their needs and goals naturally change and so too must their portfolios.

## *Early Accumulators*

*Profile*: Typically people in their early careers with long-term time horizons. Their wealth, and sometimes their income, is small relative to their debt and expenses.

*Common Goals:*

    *Short-term*   To buy a house and other essential assets.

    *Long-term*   To start a college education fund and begin saving for retirement.

### Mid-Life Consolidators

*Profile*: Typically people in their middle to late working years when
their time horizons are still relatively long. As they progress
through this phase, their income begins to exceed their expenses.

*Common Goals:*

*Short-term*   To increase their standard of living and increase their
free time.

*Long-term*   To significantly add to their retirement savings.

### Retired Spenders and Gifters

*Profile*: Typically people in retirement with declining investment time
horizons. In this phase an individual owns more assets than he or
she will ever need. To cover retirement expenses and supplement
noninvestment sources of income, assets are sometimes liquidated
and withdrawn from a portfolio. Older people will desire to gift
some of their assets to others.

*Common Goals:*

*Short-term*   To maintain their standard of living and their health
and well-being.

*Long-term*   To protect their wealth and to gift their wealth to
family and philanthropic organizations.

### Asset Allocation Suitability

Asset allocation is a critical yet simple concept that should be applied to nearly
all types of investors. Individual investors, endowments, foundations, pension and 401(k) plans, and businesses should properly allocate their portfolios. Most institutions use an asset allocation methodology in their investment
planning and management process and have done so for quite some time.

## The ABCs of Asset Classes

An *asset class* is a group of securities that share similar underlying characteristics as well as very similar risk-and-return profiles. As a result of their
similarities, the market prices of securities within each asset class tend to
move together. The market price for each security within an asset class is
highly influenced by events involving other securities within the asset class

or the asset class as a whole. Whether justified or not, even one security can greatly influence the prices for the other securities within the asset class. Asset classes are sometimes referred to as investment classes. Some of the important underlying characteristics of asset classes include the following:

- Total return potential
- Price volatility, inherent risk
- Correlations
- Growth and income trade-off
- Liquidity
- Market efficiency
- Type of issuing entity (e.g., corporation, government)

The four primary asset classes include equity assets, fixed-income assets, cash and equivalents assets, and alternative assets. Some financial experts classify cash and equivalents as fixed-income assets, while others do not. In this book I will draw a distinction between the two, although I will discuss both in the same chapter. Furthermore, some financial experts classify real estate as an asset class of its own, while others do not. Since alternative asset classes are typically comprised of hard assets and since real estate provides a hedge to equities as do the other alternative assets, I will classify them under the alternative asset class.

Each asset class can be divided into asset subclasses, such as large-cap and small-cap stocks or corporate bonds and municipal bonds. As with the primary asset classes, each asset subclass is distinguished by its own unique risk-and-return profile, together with less than perfect correlations to other asset classes. Thus, different asset subclasses enhance your portfolio's risk-and-return profile. For instance, a portfolio with both large-cap and small-cap stocks will create a more ideal risk-and-return profile than a portfolio comprised of only large-cap stocks. Asset class will be discussed further in Part Two, "Asset Class Alternatives."

• • • • • • • • • • • • • • • • • • • • • • • • • • • • • • • •

*Market Capitalization*: The total market value of a publicly traded company. Calculated by multiplying the number of shares outstanding by the market price per share.

• • • • • • • • • • • • • • • • • • • • • • • • • • • • • • • •

The process of applying asset allocation begins with identifying your specific goals and needs. These goals may include the creation of a cash emergency fund, retiring at age 60, purchasing a summer home, or taking a trip around the world upon retirement. Once your specific goals and needs have been identified, attention is given to establishing objectives and constraints.

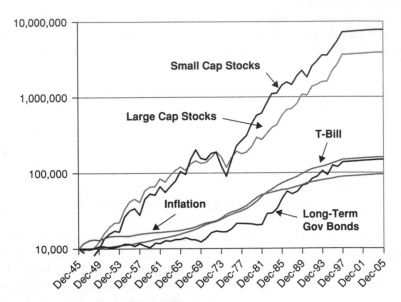

**Figure 3-3　Asset Class Historical Performance**

Your objectives and constraints are the driving force underlying the process of building and managing your portfolio. To build your optimal portfolio, you need to set SMART goals, as follows:

- *Specific*: Your goals should be unambiguous, clear, and well defined.
- *Measurable*: Your goals should be quantifiable and calculable.
- *Accepted*: Your goals should be acknowledged and motivational.
- *Realistic*: Your goals should be achievable and attainable, not lofty.
- *Time-centric*: Your goals should be for a set period, nothing indefinite.

SMART goals will help you determine which asset classes and what percentage of each to include in your portfolio. Figure 3-3 shows the performance of select asset classes. As you see, equity assets have performed the best over the period. With the highest return also comes the highest level of risk: the inescapable trade-off of risk and return.

## Moving Together with Correlation

An optimal portfolio is not just the sum of its parts. Rather, an optimal portfolio is the sum of its synergies. Synergies are created by the interaction of the asset classes held within a portfolio. This interaction is commonly referred to as *correlation* and is a critical input to the asset allocation process.

• • • • • • • • • • • • • • • • • • • • • • • • • • • • • • •

*Correlation:* The technical term used to measure and describe how closely the prices of two investments move together over time.

• • • • • • • • • • • • • • • • • • • • • • • • • • • • • • •

Positively correlated assets move in the same direction, both up and down. Conversely, negatively correlated assets move in opposite directions. Correlations between two assets are expressed on a scale between –1.0 and +1.0. The greater two assets are correlated, or move together, the closer to +1.0. Similarly, the greater two assets move in opposite directions, the closer to –1.0. Two assets that move exactly together have a +1.0 correlation whereas two assets that move exactly opposite have a –1.0 correlation.

EXAMPLE: The correlation between Stock A and Stock B is 0.8. As a result, for every $1 price movement in either stock, the other will move 80 percent in the same direction over the same time period.

Correlations between –0.3 and +0.3 are thought to be noncorrelated. This means that the two asset classes move independently of each other. With non-correlated assets, when one is rising in price, the other may be rising, falling, or maintaining its current price.

In theory, you should allocate to asset classes that are perfectly negatively correlated. However, in the real world, there are no asset classes that are perfectly negatively correlated. In reality, most asset classes are positively correlated to some degree with few exhibiting negative correlations. Given the lack of asset classes with negative correlations, focus should be on those asset classes that exhibit the lowest correlations, which are typically still positive, thus receiving some benefits of asset correlation.

Rebalancing your portfolio promotes buying low and selling high. The result is capturing the asset allocation benefit of selling potentially overvalued assets that have performed strongly and then buying potentially undervalued assets that have performed poorly. To accomplish this task, the assets in your portfolio must not move in the same way or direction. If they did, you would not be able to sell overvalued assets and buy undervalued assets. Rather, your assets would all be overvalued or all undervalued.

A properly allocated portfolio has a mix of asset classes that do not behave the same way. Correlation is therefore the measure you need to be concerned about. To maximize the portfolio benefits derived from correlations, you will need to incorporate assets with negative correlations, low positive correlations, or even assets that have noncorrelations. Noncorrelated asset classes move independently from each other. By investing in asset classes with low correlations, you are able to reduce total portfolio risk without impacting the return of your portfolio. Doing so will help to greatly minimize the overall investment-specific risk attributed to each asset class.

There is little advantage to allocating to asset classes that have high positive correlations with the asset classes already in your portfolio. Purchasing five diversified large-cap stock mutual funds will provide you with little asset allocation benefits. It is simply a waste of time.

Investments with negative correlations are extremely difficult to locate because they are very rare. Compounding the problem are constantly changing correlations, which directly impact the results of asset allocation. Correlations based on past price movements are not entirely reliable as future predictors. But since your job is not to predict the movement in correlations, allocating to asset classes with low positive correlations established over a suitable period of time is your best solution.

Also worth mentioning is that many commonly held asset class relationships are also very rare. For example, although most people are quick to point out the inverse relationship of equities and bonds, there are long periods of time when the relationship is in fact strong and moderately positively correlated.

The greatest portfolio risk reduction benefits occur during time periods when correlations across the board are low, noncorrelated, or negative. When correlations increase, risk reduction benefits are partially lost. Over time, some correlations will increase and some will decline.

Since you cannot predict which correlations will change, or to what degree they will change over time, successful investors will allocate to a number of fundamentally different asset classes to reap the benefits of asset allocation.

# Diversification 101

Diversification is not the same as asset allocation. Asset allocation involves investing in those asset classes which possess a risk-and-return profile that will achieve objectives despite constraints. On the other hand, diversification involves investing in a significant number of securities within each asset class in order to minimize investment-specific risk. Diversification focuses on minimizing risk, while asset allocation focuses on maximizing the risk-adjusted return, thus impacting both risk and return.

• • • • • • • • • • • • • • • • • • • • • • • • • • • • • • • • •

*Diversification:* A strategy designed to reduce total risk by combining a large number of securities within a particular asset class.

• • • • • • • • • • • • • • • • • • • • • • • • • • • • • • • • •

Diversification is not underscored by the trade-off between risk and return. Rather, it is underscored by the concept that adding more securities with similar risk-and-return profiles will result in lower investment-specific risk in the overall portfolio. The goal of diversification is to minimize investment-specific risk, thus leaving a portfolio with only market risk.

> EXAMPLE: If the Smith Foundation portfolio held five securities and one of those securities was negatively impacted by an investment-specific event, then 20 percent of the portfolio would be impacted. However, if the Smith Foundation held 25 securities and one of the securities was negatively impacted by an investment-specific event, then only 4 percent of the portfolio would be impacted.

Figure 3-4 illustrates the benefits of diversification. As you add more securities to your portfolio, your total risk declines. A portfolio with 20 or more securities is said to be diversified.

Only those securities with essentially the same risk-and-return profile should be used. Otherwise the risk-and-return profile of your overall portfolio will change. Obviously, finding individual securities with the same risk-and-return profiles is not easy. An alternative to finding individual securities is to purchase an index fund. You can thus achieve proper diversification without the hassle and added transaction costs from purchasing numerous securities.

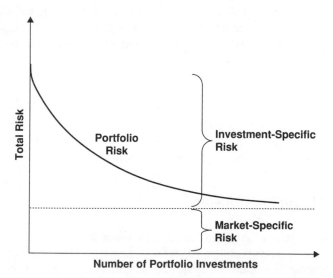

**Figure 3-4    Benefits of Portfolio Diversification**

# Time Horizon Explained

Your time horizon is another very important input variable. Most investors pay too little attention to time horizon and the important role it plays. Your time horizon affects the following:

- Expected rates of return
- Expected volatility
- Expected asset class correlations

As a result of the important role it plays, time horizon is the first constraint that should be identified. Overestimating or underestimating your time horizon can significantly impact how you allocate your assets and therefore impact your risk-and-return profile.

The primary role that time horizon plays is to help you select and evaluate the appropriateness of each asset class and asset subclass as an investment alternative. Specifically, time horizon helps to determine your balance between equity investments and fixed-income investments. The shorter your time horizon, the more emphasis you should place on fixed-income investments. Conversely, the longer your time horizon, the more emphasis you should place on equity investments. In the short term, equities are simply too volatile and possess high levels of uncertainty. In other words, equities exhibit unacceptable levels of risk in relation to their expected returns. On the other hand, fixed-income investments are significantly less volatile in the short term and possess much lower levels of uncertainty. As a consequence, fixed-income risks in relation to their expected returns are more favorable in the short term.

As your investment time horizon increases, so too does the probability that your equity assets will experience positive returns. Over longer periods of time, equity returns become more stable as there is more time for positive equity returns to offset negative equity returns. The returns of equities become significantly clearer and more predictable as your investment time horizon lengthens. Figures 3-5 and 3-6 illustrate this point.

# Asset Allocation Strategies

Determining your asset allocation strategy is almost as important as determining your optimal asset mix. Asset allocation strategies are the foundation of rebalancing, one of the cornerstone principles of asset allocation.

| Investment<br>Holding Period | Probability of Equities<br>Outperforming Fixed-Income |
|:---:|:---:|
| 1 Year | > 60% |
| 3 Years | > 70% |
| 5 Years | > 75% |
| 10 Years | > 90% |
| 25 Years | > 99% |

**Figure 3-5   Equities versus Fixed Income**

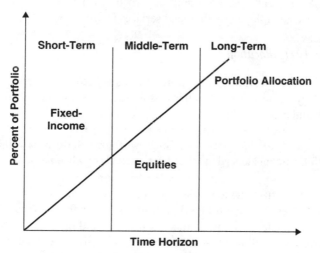

**Figure 3-6   Time Horizon and Portfolio Balance**

. . . . . . . . . . . . . . . . . . . . . . . . . . . . . . . .

*Rebalancing*: The process of returning the current asset mix to the target asset mix by selling overallocated asset classes and buying underallocated asset classes.

. . . . . . . . . . . . . . . . . . . . . . . . . . . . . . . .

There are a number of different asset allocation strategies available to you. Some are more common whereas others are the inventions and proprietary use of financial services firms. The two most common strategies in use by the financial community are strategic and tactical, but many investment managers employee some combination of the two.

Two other well-known but less employed strategies are integrated asset allocation and insured asset allocation. Although they will not be covered in this book, you should know what they are. *Integrated asset allocation* is a strategy whereby you periodically change your optimal asset mix depending on changes to either your objectives and constraints or market conditions. This strategy is essentially a combination of strategic asset allocation and tactical asset allocation. *Insured asset allocation* is a strategy whereby you change your optimal asset mix in response to your changing risk tolerance, which is thought to rise as you age and accumulate more wealth. As a result, your allocation to equities rises at the expense of cash and equivalents. In addition, your optimal asset mix could change to include a greater allocation to cash and equivalents if the total market value of your portfolio declined due to market weakness. Let's shift our focus to the two asset allocation strategies most employed by financial services firms.

## Strategic Asset Allocation

Strategic asset allocation can be thought of as a passive long-term strategy. This strategy is appropriate for all investors and under all market conditions, both bull and bear.

· · · · · · · · · · · · · · · · · · · · · · · · · · · · · ·

*Strategic Asset Allocation*: A strategy whereby asset classes within a portfolio are rebalanced at select time intervals or when needed.

· · · · · · · · · · · · · · · · · · · · · · · · · · · · · ·

Do not confuse strategic asset allocation with the philosophy of *buy and hold*. Under the buy-and-hold philosophy, a portfolio is created and no revisions are made to the asset mix during the holding period. Over time, price movements will alter—sometimes substantially—the asset mix of the portfolio. As a result, the portfolio will either exhibit greater risk than appropriate since the portfolio is overallocated to one asset class or experience a lower than expected return since the portfolio does not receive the return enhancing benefits derived from multiclass investing. Market weakness will have a magnified effect since some asset classes will be disproportionately too large given no rebalancing. As you can see, a buy-and-hold strategy conflicts with the underlying philosophy of rebalancing.

When designing your portfolio, the appropriate asset classes are first selected followed by their optimal weightings. Over time, the price of each asset class fluctuates, either up or down, depending on market forces. As a result, the asset class weightings will change. For instance, if fixed-income prices experience significant strength, then the fixed-income allocation, as a percentage of the overall portfolio, will increase. At the same time, the other asset class allocations, as percentages of the overall portfolio, will decline.

> EXAMPLE: A portfolio was designed with an optimal asset mix of 60 percent equities, 30 percent fixed-income, and 10 percent cash and equivalents. Due to a surge in equity prices, one year later the portfolio was comprised of 75 percent equities, 20 percent fixed-income, and 5 percent cash and equivalents. Under strategic asset allocation, the portfolio manager will sell equities, or approximately 15 percent (75 – 60) of the portfolio market value, and reinvest the proceeds in fixed-income and cash and equivalents. Doing so will return the portfolio to the optimal asset mix.

Portfolio managers often establish asset class allocation ranges via floors and ceilings. As long as asset class weightings move within their respective allocation ranges, portfolio managers generally will take no action. However, if an asset class weighting moves above the ceiling or below the floor, a portfolio manager will generally rebalance the portfolio.

> EXAMPLE: A portfolio has an optimal asset mix of 50 percent equities, 40 percent fixed-income, and 10 percent cash and equivalents. The portfolio manager establishes an equity ceiling at 60 percent and a floor at 40 percent. One year later the equity weighting reaches 61 percent. In response, the portfolio manager sells equities equal to 11 percent (61 – 50) of the portfolio value and buys fixed-income and cash and equivalents, thus returning the portfolio to the optimal asset mix.

## Tactical Asset Allocation

Tactical asset allocation is a form of market timing. The goal is to capture higher returns by capitalizing on short-term price movements. Tactical asset allocation is founded on the notion that the market is to some degree inefficient and that skillful portfolio managers can profit from these inefficiencies. In other words, this strategy attempts to "beat the market."

• • • • • • • • • • • • • • • • • • • • • • • • • • • • • •

*Tactical Asset Allocation*: A market timing strategy where the asset mix is intentionally changed with the hope of capturing short-term profits from changing asset class prices.

• • • • • • • • • • • • • • • • • • • • • • • • • • • • • •

Under this strategy, asset classes are deliberately changed in response to current and anticipated future asset class price movements. Contrary to strategic asset allocation, under tactical asset allocation, an asset class showing strength may be allowed to "run," so-to-speak, by adjusting the optimal asset mix. In doing so, the hope is to profit from the increasing price.

With tactical asset allocation, portfolio managers employ a number of different methods to find market inefficiencies and to determine when and how to profit from them. One of the most common methods is to analyze the business cycle and create a forecast based on multiple possible future economic scenarios. The result of this forecast is then used to produce expected returns for each asset class. Comparisons of their expected returns for each asset class are measured against market expectations.

Although this strategy is an asset allocation strategy, remember that the focus of tactical asset allocation is to profit from market timing. As we know, market timing determines only a small fraction of total investment performance over time.

Personally, I am a proponent of strategic asset allocation. I employ it at my firm and suggest you consider using it as well. By selecting tactical asset allocation, you are simply betting that you can beat the market.

In the next chapter, you will learn about asset allocation under the microscope—the 10 cornerstone principles of asset allocation.

C H A P T E R

# The 10 Cornerstone Principles of Asset Allocation

Principles can be described as the beginning, the foundation, the source, or the essence upon which things build and expand. Principles represent pure knowledge and fundamental parameters and guidelines. As such, I have assembled the most important principles underlying asset allocation, or those that I refer to as the cornerstone principles, to better help you understand and conceptualize asset allocation.

I call these the cornerstone principles because asset allocation is so firmly grounded in and reliant on them. Each principle plays a necessary and indeed vital role in establishing and maintaining a truly optimal asset allocation. By practicing the 10 cornerstone principles of asset allocation, you will be able to build the most appropriate portfolio for your situation.

The 10 cornerstone principles can be categorized into four master groups, each having unique impacts on the asset allocation process and on decision making. The four master groups include the following:

- *Market-Specific*: Cornerstone Principle 1
- *Investor-Specific*: Cornerstone Principles 2, 3, and 4

- *Investment-Specific*: Cornerstone Principles 5, 6, and 7
- *Portfolio-Specific*: Cornerstone Principles 8, 9, and 10

# Cornerstone Principle 1: Market Efficiency

Market efficiency is the golden principle of all asset allocation cornerstone principles. Without some degree of market efficiency, we would not employ asset allocation and would probably focus instead on security selection. Fortunately, our financial markets are highly efficient and are becoming even more so as information technology gets better with time.

Underlying asset allocation are two highly influential and well-known investment concepts. These are the modern portfolio theory (MPT) and the efficient market hypothesis (EMH), which is essentially a refinement of the modern portfolio theory.

Modern portfolio theory says that neither investors nor portfolio managers should evaluate each investment on a stand-alone basis. But rather they should evaluate each investment based on its true ability to enhance the overall risk-and-return trade-off profile of a portfolio. Moreover, modern portfolio theory states that when an investor is faced with two investments with identical expected returns, but different levels of risk, that investor would be wise to select the investment that has the lower risk. This sounds quite simple and easy to follow, doesn't it? The same theory, viewed from a slightly different angle, says that a rational investor would be wise to select the investment with the higher return when faced with two investments that have different expected returns, but identical levels of risk.

Lastly, modern portfolio theory introduces and emphasizes the must-know concept of correlation, and stresses—when employed properly—how it can enhance the risk-and-return trade-off profile of a portfolio, thus driving portfolio performance.

The efficient market hypothesis, in a related way, says that security prices are fair and reasonable because they fully reflect all available public and non-public information that might affect them. As a result, security selection and market timing are presupposed to failure over the long term since every investor has the same, or nearly the same, information. As a result, it is the amount of risk that investors are willing to accept that explains their real investment performance over time. Contrary to a common misconception, the efficient market hypothesis does not say that it is impossible to beat the performance of the market. Over any time period, there will be some investors who will beat the market and those who will not. The weight is squarely with those who will not beat the market. The number of investors who beat the market in any particular time period will be relatively no greater than expected by standard mathematical probability. Statistical outliers are highly common in the world of investment performance. This fact is simply the numerical law of large numbers.

## Cornerstone Principle 2: Investor Risk Profile

Your optimal portfolio is designed based principally on your willingness, ability, and need to tolerate risk. Consequently, once your risk tolerance is determined, your optimal asset mix can then be established in order to maximize your portfolio's return potential. This concept is expressed as the risk-and-return trade-off profile. The best method to identify your risk tolerance is to complete a risk assessment questionnaire followed by a face-to-face discussion of risk with your financial advisor. Personal preferences toward risk assumption play a vital role in determining your willingness to tolerate risk, and a face-to-face conversation will help you to learn more about this. For example, two different investors with the same level of wealth and the same specific goals and needs would each have a different preference for assuming risk. Factors such as occupation, sex, age, and education have been shown to influence an investor's tolerance for assuming risk.

Your ability to tolerate risk is highly contingent on your investment time horizon and level of wealth. All else being equal, the longer your investment time horizon and the greater your level of wealth, the more risk you are able to tolerate. Why? Intuitively one can see how people with longer time horizons and people with greater levels of wealth have more room for error in achieving their specific goals and needs. Of course this is not always the case, but as a general rule it usually holds true.

In practice, there are four stages of wealth building, or what are referred to as life-cycle phases. These include the accumulation phase, consolidation phase, spending phase, and gifting phase. Most people begin their investing lives in the accumulation phase, and by the time they are well into their golden years they are in the gifting phase.

## Cornerstone Principle 3: SMART Financial Goals

Asset allocation is the strategy of dividing the assets within a portfolio among the different asset classes to achieve the highest expected total rate of return for the level of risk you are willing and able to accept. As a result, knowing why you are investing and what you are attempting to accomplish is the vital first step. You cannot hit a target you are not aiming for.

When identifying your specific goals and needs, focus on quantifying and prioritizing them. Simply saying you need enough money to fund a college education or support yourself in retirement is much too ambiguous and not especially intelligent. Identifying that you need $25,000 per year for four years in tomorrow's dollars or $75,000 per year in retirement expressed in today's dollars is more appropriate. Lastly, when identifying your specific goals and needs, ensure that they are realistic, achievable, and measurable. For example, determining that you need a 25 percent annual return for 20 years to accumulate $2,000,000 for retirement is measurable, but far from realistic and achievable.

Once you establish your specific goals and needs, you are then able to create the portfolio's risk-and-return trade-off profile: see Cornerstone Principle 6.

## Cornerstone Principle 4: Time Horizon

Time horizon plays a significant role in estimating asset class returns, risk levels, and price correlations. As mentioned in other cornerstone principles, accurate forecasts are essential to building an optimal portfolio. The primary use of time horizon is to help determine the portfolio balance between equity assets and assets that emphasize current income, namely fixed-income and cash and equivalents. All else being equal, the longer your investment time horizon, the more equity investments and less current income-producing investments you should incorporate. Conversely, the shorter your investment time horizon, the more current income-producing investments and less equity investments you should incorporate.

The most common risk that will need to be addressed over the long term is purchasing power risk, or the loss of an asset's real value due to inflation. Equity investments provide the best hedge against this risk. As a result, the longer your investment time horizon, the more you should allocate to equity assets. In the short term, the most common risk is volatility risk. Fixed-income investments provide the best hedge against this type of risk and so should be emphasized in your portfolio as well.

## Cornerstone Principle 5: Expected Total Return

Expected total return is simply your forecast of total return for each asset class and asset subclass during the future holding period. Using historical rates of return in lieu of estimating expected rates is not only quick and easy but also a prudent approach used by many financial professionals.

Once your risk tolerance has been identified, you then design your portfolio to maximize your expected total rate of return for the given level of risk you are willing, able, and need to assume. This task cannot be accomplished without an estimate of future returns. This is the essence of the risk-and-return trade-off profile. Without a clear understanding of expected total rates of return for each asset class, there is little hope of maximizing a portfolio's performance and building your optimal portfolio.

## Cornerstone Principle 6: Risk-and-Return Trade-off Profile

The trade-off between investment-specific risk and return is central to the application of asset allocation theory to an investment portfolio. Risk and return are unequivocally linked, and one simply cannot earn an excessive return while assuming a corresponding low risk. In basic asset allocation theory, the higher your risk tolerance, the higher your potential return. You should not assume higher risk for the same potential return that a less risky asset may offer. The message here is that you need to build a portfolio with the maximum expected total rate of return given the level of risk you are willing, able, and need to assume.

This cornerstone principle is derived from the efficient market hypothesis and modern portfolio theory, the two celebrated investment theories already mentioned.

## Cornerstone Principle 7: Correlation

The term *correlation* refers to how closely the market prices of two investments, or, in the case of asset allocation, the prices of two asset classes move in relation to each other. Although not always the case, most securities within an asset class or asset subclass tend to move together over time. Of course, there are always exceptions.

Your aim is to allocate investments to asset classes and asset subclasses that do not move in perfect lockstep with each other. The greater the difference or the lower the correlation that two asset classes move together, the more attractive they are for investment purposes. Since some asset classes experience strength at one time whereas others experience strength at other times, it may be appropriate, depending on your tolerance for risk, to allocate among multiple asset classes at all times. Investing in multiple asset classes allows you to avoid serious market and portfolio weakness. Lastly, by investing in multiple asset classes with low correlations, you enhance the risk-and-return trade-off profile for your portfolio.

## Cornerstone Principle 8: Diversification

It is important to apply the principle of diversification in order to minimize risk in a portfolio. As noted earlier, diversification is not the same as asset allocation, and the two concepts should not be confused.

The task of diversifying a portfolio should be addressed after completing the process of allocating among asset classes and asset subclasses. *Diversification* is the process of investing in a significant number of not-too-similar investments within each asset class in order to reduce, if not eliminate altogether, the risk associated with each individual investment, namely investment-specific risk. By holding a significant number of not-too-similar investments, the impact resulting from a negative investment-specific event will be minimized. To achieve the greatest benefits, investors should diversify all of their holdings (equities, fixed-income, real estate, commodities, etc.) and not just select asset classes or asset subclasses. However, due to the significant level of inherent investment-specific risk, diversification will provide the greatest benefit to the equity portion of a portfolio.

It is important to understand that the process of diversification entails investing in a significant number of not-too-similar investments with *similar* risk-and-return trade-off profiles. In doing so, your risk-and-return trade-off profile will remain constant. Investing in broad market index funds provides a reliable solution for gaining diversification quickly and easily. Low-cost and tax-efficient exchange-traded funds are most ideal in the author's opinion.

## Cornerstone Principle 9: Optimal Asset Mix

Asset mix refers to both the asset classes and asset subclasses that a portfolio is allocated to and their respective weightings within that portfolio. It is essential to allocate a portfolio's assets in a deliberate and calculated way in order to develop the desired risk-and-return trade-off profile. Thus, allocating assets to those asset classes and asset subclasses to develop the desired risk-and-return trade-off profile defines the optimal asset mix.

Incorrectly allocating assets will create a situation where the portfolio either assumes more risk than appropriate or does not assume enough risk, thereby depriving you of better returns. As you know, your work does not stop once your portfolio is designed and built. Constant monitoring and rebalancing will need to take place. Rebalancing, Cornerstone Principle 10, is important to keep the asset mix in balance with the optimal asset mix.

# Cornerstone Principle 10: Reoptimization

Over time, a portfolio's asset mix, including the resulting risk-and-return trade-off profile, will change due to price fluctuations, with some fluctuations being quite large. To address this issue, reoptimization may be appropriate and needed. Reoptimization is comprised of four different, but somewhat similar, tasks. These tasks, or what I term the Four Rs of Reoptimization, include *reevaluating, rebalancing, relocating,* and *reallocating.*

Reevaluating is the task of examining recent changes in your life and evaluating them within the context of your portfolio. Many things may have changed in your life since you last designed and built your portfolio, and these could impact your SMART financial goals and risk profile. As a result, you should take a long, hard look at your original financial plan and portfolio and modify them if needed.

Rebalancing is the task of selling and buying investments in order to return a portfolio's current asset class mix to the previously established optimal asset mix. Rebalancing involves selling a portion of those asset classes that have become overweighted and buying a portion of those asset classes that have become underweighted.

Relocating is the task of exchanging certain assets for other assets without changing the overall asset mix or risk-and-return trade-off profile. Relocating might involve exchanging a certain bond to obtain a higher or lower current rate of income depending on how your need for income has changed.

Reallocating is the task of adjusting to which investments your contributions go and in what amount. In this context, reallocating does not change the mix of your assets, only how contributions will be made in the future.

---

In the next chapter, you will learn about equity investments, the asset class that offers the highest return potential, but also the highest risk potential.

# PART TWO

# ASSET CLASS ALTERNATIVES

5

# Equity Investments: Higher Return, *but* Higher Risk Assets

## Overview of Equity Assets

Over 150 million Americans own stock either directly or indirectly via mutual funds, index funds, managed accounts, or some insurance products. The number of Americans owning equities has ballooned over the last couple of decades, and the trend continues to rise. Private retirement accounts could push this number even higher as people begin to invest their money themselves in the financial markets rather than have the government do so.

Equity assets are typically the core of traditional investment portfolios. Equities can be divided into specific fundamentally different categories, such as size, style (growth or value), and industry. Each fundamental difference provides greater investment opportunities and more ways to enhance your overall portfolio. The term used to describe this gain is *premium*.

Although we will be focusing on equities exclusively in this chapter, note that not all equities are the same or highly correlated. This is the result of inherent fundamental differences. During some time periods, some types of equities will perform well, whereas at other times other equities will perform well. For instance, during economic recessions, consumer staple stocks, or the stocks of those companies that produce products we need regardless of how well the economy is doing (toothpaste, shaving razors, toilet paper, pet food), will outpace consumer nonstaple stocks. This second group encompasses companies that sell products or services that are considered to be more discretionary in nature, such as premium foods, fancy wines, and music CDs. However, during economic recovery and expansion, consumer nonstaple stocks will outperform consumer staple stocks.

Equity assets represent an ownership interest in a corporation and signify a claim to a corporation's assets. In order to fund business operations, corporations first raise capital by issuing equity securities. Each share of stock owned gives an investor a proportional share of the corporation's profits, which are usually distributed in the form of dividends. In addition, owners of most equity securities are given voting rights. Voting rights allow you, for instance, to vote for a corporation's board of directors, approve or disapprove employee stock option programs, and vote for or against acquisitions. From my experience, individual investors foolishly do not exercise their right to vote. In response, more power shifts to corporate management shareholders and to large institutions. Each of these groups has their own agenda, which typically isn't always on the same page as individual investors. Remember to always exercise your right to vote.

## Framework of Equity Assets

Today you can find over 8,000 companies that trade in the United States with about half of those companies listed on a national stock exchange, such as the New York Stock Exchange (NYSE), American Stock Exchange (Amex), and the Nasdaq, or the National Association of Securities Dealers Automatic Quote System. The NYSE lists over 1,500 companies while the Nasdaq and Amex list over 3,000 and nearly 400, respectively. On a market value basis, the NYSE comprises about 80 percent of the aggregate U.S. market value. The Nasdaq comprises about 19 percent with the Amex comprising less than 1 percent. These listings do not include exchange-traded funds (ETFs), foreign stocks, or preferred stocks. It is safe to say that the breadth and depth of investment options is quite extensive.

There are essentially two types of equity securities: preferred stock and common stock. Common stock is much more widely held than preferred stock, and there is a sizable difference between the two. Do not get caught up in the name of each type of equity stock. Owning preferred stock is not necessarily more desirable even though the name sounds better. Each offers their own benefits, and each is suitable for different types of investors. We will first explore preferred stock and then common stock.

## Preferred Stock

Preferred stock represents ownership of a corporation, but it is slightly different from common stock. Preferred stock shareholders do not have voting rights. In exchange, shareholders receive a higher priority on the assets of the corporation in the event of liquidation due to bankruptcy. Furthermore, it is commonplace for shareholders of preferred stock to receive not only a higher yielding dividend but also priority in receiving dividends over that of common stock shareholders. For example, if a corporation is having difficulty in meeting their dividend payments to both preferred and common stock shareholders, the corporation must make dividend payments to the preferred stock shareholders first. Afterward, provided enough cash remains, common stock shareholders will receive their dividend payments.

· · · · · · · · · · · · · · · · · · · · · · · · · · · · · · ·

*Cumulative Preferred*: A type of preferred stock that has priority in receiving dividends over that of common stock. The cumulative provision obligates the corporation to pay all accumulated dividends before dividends can be made to the shareholders of common stock.

· · · · · · · · · · · · · · · · · · · · · · · · · · · · · · ·

Lastly, many corporations issue what is called *convertible preferred stock*. This type of preferred is very similar to nonconvertible preferred stock with one significant difference. Convertible preferred stock gives the owner the option to convert, or exchange, his or her preferred shares into a fixed number of common stock shares after a predetermined date. The market value of this type of preferred is more volatile since its value is influenced by the market value of the related common stock.

## Common Stock

Common stock is the most widely used form of equity ownership. Common stock shareholders have voting rights and often receive profits in the form of dividends. However, not all corporations distribute profits in the form of dividends. Rather, some reinvest the dividends back into the company in order to fund existing and planned operations.

Two of the most common asset subclass groups are *equity style* and *equity size*. Style refers to a certain stock as being growth or value, whereas size refers to a certain stock as being large-cap, medium-cap, small-cap, or even micro-cap. Both of these asset subclasses have similar characteristics with each other since they both are equity securities. However, they also have very important differences, which possess their own unique risk-and-return trade-off profiles. Growth stocks are considered stocks of companies that produce higher rates of return than do stocks of their industry peers. Value stocks, on the other hand, are stocks that are considered undervalued given their expected rates of return and current stock prices. As a result of the differences between style stocks and size stocks, their correlation with each other tends to be somewhat lower and therefore provide diversification benefits.

Morningstar employs the following factors and analysis weights to define and classify stocks as value stocks:

- Stock Price to Projected Earnings: 50 percent
- Stock Price to Book Value per Share: 12.5 percent
- Stock Price to Sales per Share: 12.5 percent
- Stock Price to Cash Flow per Share: 12.5 percent
- Dividend yield: 12.5 percent

To define and classify stocks as growth stocks, Morningstar uses the following factors and weightings:

- Long-term Estimated Earnings Growth: 50 percent
- Historical Earnings Growth Rate: 12.5 percent
- Sales Growth: 12.5 percent
- Cash Flow Growth: 12.5 percent
- Book Value Growth: 12.5 percent

Depending on the value for each factor, Morningstar will assign a particular stock as either growth, value, or core. Core stocks are essentially balanced stocks that do not exhibit material growth or value tendencies. These rankings by Morningstar are the backbone of their stock and mutual fund star-ranking system.

Intuitively, one can see how a particular security can be considered a value stock at one point in time and then be considered a growth stock at a later point in time as the price of the security advances. Since growth and value stocks do not move in perfect lockstep with each other, investors have the opportunity to improve the risk-adjusted return of their portfolio by allocating to both asset classes. Low-cost ETFs are excellent ways to accomplish this task.

## Most Common Equity Types

- Large market capitalization
- Middle market capitalization

- Small market capitalization
- Micromarket capitalization
- Growth style
- Value style
- Master limited partnerships
- Venture capital
- Developed international markets
- Emerging international markets

## Factors Influencing Equity Returns

- Overall market conditions
- Investment-specific characteristics, principally the present value of expected future cash flows
- Valuations, as measured by price to sales, price to earnings, price to free cash flow, and price to tangible book value
- Investors' behaviors, preferences, and risk tolerances
- Flow of funds

## Positives and Negatives of Equities

### Positives

- High total return potential
- Participation in capital appreciation and voting as a result of stock ownership
- Availability of numerous asset subclasses to enhance the risk-and-return trade-off profile and to satisfy different investor preferences
- Liquid and efficient markets
- A hedge against inflation risk
- Ease of diversification

### Negatives

- Potential for high risk
- High volatility risk
- Low current income potential (dividends)
- Difficult to forecast risk and return
- Fluctuating correlations

- Potential for high management fees
- International currency or political risks

## Historical Performance

The performance of equities is truly across the board. During some time periods in the past, equities have performed quite nicely whereas during other time periods, equities have performed quite poorly. For example, the period 2000–2004 saw the total stock market decline by nearly 5 percent; whereas during the time period 1968–1982, the total stock market advanced by 0.2 percent. Not a strong return, but different from the 2000–2004 time period and positive nevertheless.

Historically, the total stock market has returned slightly over 12 percent annually for the period 1950 to the end of 2005. This annual return compares rather favorably to both U.S. Treasury notes and U.S. inflation, advancing 6.2 and 3.9 percent annually during the same time period. Always keep in mind that equities have outpaced inflation and to a lesser degree fixed-income investments over time—and sometimes to a superior margin.

## Equity Volatility Risk

There is little doubt that equity assets possess the greatest amount of risk of all asset classes. Moreover, some equity asset classes exhibit greater amounts of risk than other equity asset classes. For example, smaller capitalization stocks possess more risk than larger capitalization stocks. However, with more risk comes more return potential. The two go hand in hand, and one surely cannot earn a high return without assuming a corresponding level of risk.

Historically, small-cap stocks have experienced the greatest volatility risk. From the mid-1950s to the mid-2000s, small-cap stocks have exhibited a standard deviation of nearly 20 percent. Now that's substantial! Large- and mid-cap also have volatility risk, but tend to experience less volatility given their developed companies. Conversely, micro-cap stocks behave somewhat similar to small-cap stocks in that their price tends to fluctuate greatly. That could spell problems depending on your risk profile: your risk tolerance, risk capacity, and risk need.

By allocating to investments that possess low correlations, you can reduce portfolio volatility and smooth out the large price swings. Adding more investments to your portfolio will cut volatility and price swings by an even greater amount.

# Equity Correlations

Equity asset classes typically have high correlations with each other. Large-cap stocks have a correlation of close to 0.75 with small-cap stocks during the period since 1926. Mid-cap stocks, on the other hand, have even closer correlations to large-cap stocks. Regardless, the differential in correlations does provide enhancements to the risk-adjusted return. The greatest differential in correlations is with short-term fixed-income investments, namely Treasury bills and shortened Treasury notes. Your objective is to allocate to asset classes that have low correlations with one another. Doing so will enhance the risk-and-return trade-off profile of your portfolio.

# Portfolio Enhancement Opportunities

Much research has been done in the area of what drives portfolio returns from both a macro and micro standpoint. Asset allocation has been clearly shown to be the primary determinant of portfolio performance over time. But what about the variables that also drive performance from a micro level? The following are three variables that have been shown to determine a significant level of performance and provide you with solid investment options. You should consider each very carefully within the context of your personal situation.

## *Volatility Premium*

The greater the level of risk, the greater the potential for a higher return. This is the essence of investing. Remember that there are no shortcuts. One method for evaluating volatility is with beta. *Beta* is a financial measurement designed to illustrate the movement of a particular stock in relation to the overall market. The greater a beta, the greater the price movement, and therefore the greater the potential for risk and return. Respected research has concluded that nearly 70 percent of portfolio returns are driven by beta. As a result, allocating to high beta investments in partnership with a solid asset allocation and diversification plan will help to enhance the risk-adjusted return in your portfolio. High beta investments can be found in nearly all stock market cap groups; however, research has shown that smaller investments typically have higher betas. If you can tolerate the large price swings, gaining this size premium could be a very wise move. Usually only small-cap and micro-cap stocks offer sizable premium benefits.

One final word about the volatility premium. Beta is not the only measurement for volatility; thus you may find it more convenient to measure risk
a different way so as to incorporate only those stocks with high volatilities.
Standard deviation is another measurement that could be used.

## Style Premium

Simply put, *style* refers to either a growth or value stock. Each classification is defined by very specific factors and provides different portfolio benefits as a result. Many years ago, dividend yield and book value were the
primary determinants for classifying stocks as growth or value. Over time,
additional research was done and now we have more sophisticated methods
for classification.

Over the same time period, research was done into what type of stock,
either growth or value, outperformed the other. Most research clearly shows
that value stocks outpace growth stocks over time to the tune of several percentage points. Moreover, these findings also show that volatility risk is lower
for value stocks than for growth stocks. In consequence, value stocks provide
a means to enhance your portfolio return while also providing a means to
reduce total portfolio risk. A very nice combination, indeed. Unfortunately,
the higher return does come with higher risk. During the period from 1929 to
1932, small caps as a whole lost over 85 percent of their real value.

Although the correlations between growth and value stocks are quite
high, there have been periods when the correlations have come under siege.
During the late 1990s, correlations declined to nearly 0.5, still materially
positive but offering solid allocation benefits. As a result of this research,
investing in value stocks could be a smart move.

## Size Premium

The size of a particular stock, or broad market index tracking those stocks,
can provide portfolio enhancement opportunities. The *size* of a stock is measured by what is called *market capitalization*. This is measured by taking the
outstanding stock of a particular company and multiplying it by the price of
the stock. Thus you arrive at an identifiable total market value for a company that can then be classified into a definable group. Note that the new
trend for calculating market capitalization is to replace total outstanding
stock with what is called *free float* shares outstanding. Free float refers to
the total shares outstanding less what is held by private ownership, such as
corporate insiders. Doing so will provide a better picture of a company available to the investing public.

• • • • • • • • • • • • • • • • • • • • • • • • • • • • • •

*Market Capitalization*: Measured by taking the outstanding stock of a particular company and multiplying it by the price of the stock.

• • • • • • • • • • • • • • • • • • • • • • • • • • • • • •

*Free Float*: Refers to the total shares outstanding less what is held by private ownership, such as corporate insiders.

• • • • • • • • • • • • • • • • • • • • • • • • • • • • • •

The four size categories are large-cap, mid-cap, small-cap, and micro-cap stocks. Large-cap stocks comprise roughly 70 percent of all investable stocks while mid-cap, small-cap, and micro-cap stocks comprise 20 percent, 7 percent, and 2 percent, respectively.

Research has demonstrated that small-cap stocks have outperformed large-cap stocks over time. More specifically, micro-cap stocks have outpaced large-cap stocks by a wide margin, even after adjusting for volatility. In addition, micro-cap stocks were found to sometimes buck the equity trends and move differently than the total stock market. Thus, there is an enhancement opportunity with smaller size companies.

In summary, equity size does matter and can provide return enhancement and risk reduction benefits. Small-cap and micro-cap stocks should be highly considered when designing your portfolio.

## Portfolio Allocation Considerations

Equity assets are the backbone of most well-diversified optimal portfolios. Equities provide the best way to defend against purchasing power risk, or the loss of asset value due to the corrosive impact of inflation. To gain portfolio enhancement benefits, you should consider allocating a portion of your assets to small-cap stocks and possibly micro-cap stocks as well. In addition, allocating to value stocks could be a wise decision to further enhance your portfolio. A combination of the two will provide for a quick and easy method of benefiting your portfolio. Small-cap value index funds are available, as are micro-cap index funds. Stacking of investment option premiums is ideal.

## Investment Options

Figure 5-1 provides some investment options you may want to consider for your own portfolio. As a strong proponent of index funds, I have only included low-cost and highly diversified index funds with an emphasis on exchange-traded funds. I strongly encourage you to evaluate the list in Figure 5-1 and

| Index Fund | Symbol |
|---|---|
| iShares Total U.S. Stock Market | IYY |
| Vanguard Total U.S. Stock Market | VTSMX |
| NYSE Composite | NYC |
| iShares Russell 3000 | IVV |
| iShares S&P 1500 | ISI |
| iShares S&P SmallCap 600 Value | IJS |
| Morningstar Small Value | JKL |
| Vanguard Small Value | VISVX |
| iShares Russell MicroCap | IWC |
| Bridgeway Ultra Small Company | BRSIX |

**Figure 5-1    Select Equity Investment Options**

determine for yourself if these investment options make sense for your needs. Depending on your financial situation and goals, you may want to incorporate a number of these or simply use one or two. The list is divided into multiple asset subclasses, each offering portfolio risk-and-return premium enhancement opportunities.

In the next chapter, you will learn about fixed-income investments, the path to lower risk potential, yet offering lower return potential at the same time.

6

# Fixed-Income
# Investments:
# Lower Risk, *but*
# Lower Return Assets

## Bonding with Fixed-Income

Given the scope of the fixed-income market, you have many opportunities to locate and invest in a fixed-income investment that will provide you with asset allocation benefits. There are many kinds of fixed-income categories from mortgage-backed bonds to corporate bonds and from government bonds to foreign bonds. The market is truly expansive. Each one of these categories exhibits different risk-and-return potential. Allocating to a diversified fixed-income investment is an ideal way to enhance your total portfolio risk-adjusted return.

The simplest and best method for investing in fixed-income is through a low-cost bond index fund or mutual fund. Doing so will provide you with immediate exposure to the overall fixed-income market with a highly diversified and low-cost investment. Using an index fund in place of direct purchases is ideal when the investment category is complex, such as high-yield corporate bonds. Spreading the risk from one particular bond across a pool of bonds will ensure that you do not experience excessive losses. One excellent bond exchange-traded fund that is used at my company is the Lehman Aggregate Bond Fund, symbol AGG. This ETF provides a decent interest yield and has the potential for price appreciation under certain market conditions. There are other bond index funds to select from as well.

Technically speaking, a *fixed-income investment* represents a loan to a corporation or governmental entity in order to raise capital to finance many different kinds of expenditures. In the investment community, fixed-income assets are commonly referred to as bonds or debt. In most cases, assets of the issuer back each fixed-income security, thus providing the purchaser with some protection in the case of default. These assets, or debt instruments, hold the issuer to a contractual obligation to make periodic interest payments to the purchaser on predetermined dates in predetermined amounts until the security reaches maturity or is called by the issuer.

· · · · · · · · · · · · · · · · · · · · · · · · · · · · · ·

*Maturity*: The date on which an issuer is obligated to pay the principal of a fixed-income security to the purchaser.

· · · · · · · · · · · · · · · · · · · · · · · · · · · · · ·

*Called*: An event where a fixed-income security is redeemed by the issuer prior to maturity.

· · · · · · · · · · · · · · · · · · · · · · · · · · · · · ·

Typically, the longer the time to maturity for a fixed-income security, the higher its yield. Thus, short-term securities tend to have lower yields than do long-term securities. This is not always the case, but tends to hold true for the vast majority of time. The yield is the annual rate of return for a fixed-income investment derived from dividing the annual interest payments by the purchase price or market value (depending on when and how you are evaluating the security). Cash and equivalents do have many similarities with fixed-income securities; however, the one characteristic that defines them as cash and equivalents rather than fixed-income is their short-term maturity. But why do securities with longer maturities have higher yields? The principal and most accepted theory—since there are other theories—says that investors demand higher rates of return for each progressively longer period of time because they must forgo current consumption of the money they invest and assume risk for a longer period of time. Bond issuers know they need to increase the interest rate on long-term investments to entice investors.

To illustrate how investors demand higher rates of return for securities with longer maturities, the yield curve was created. A *yield curve* is the graphical representation of the relationship between fixed-income yields and their time to maturity. Under normal economic conditions, yield curves are upward sloping; thus the yields increase as the time to maturity increases. This is known as a *normal* yield curve. When the yields for both short-term and long-term bonds are the same, the yield curve is said to be *flat*. However, when the yields on long-term bonds arc lower than the yields on short-term bonds, the yield curve is said to be *inverted*.

Although considered a separate asset class from fixed-income investment, cash and equivalents assets are a very broad category defining those assets that are highly liquid, very safe, and can be converted easily into cash, such as money market funds or coins and bills. Cash and equivalents usually have a maturity date within one year. The returns of this asset class generally correlate to the rate of inflation. Thus, as inflation rates fall, so too do the rates on money market funds and certificates of deposit. Cash and equivalents are differentiated by their issuer, maturity date, interest rate (referred to as coupon rate), credit quality, and tax status (taxable or nontaxable).

# Framework of Fixed-Income Assets

Fixed-income investments are available in a wide variety of categories. Each category is different from the next, which is good since your goal is to invest in assets that are fundamentally different from one another. Four of the primary factors impacting most investors' decisions when evaluating fixed-income investments include tax considerations, length of maturity, credit and default risk, or the uncertainty that an issuer will be able to make required interest payments or principal payments at maturity.

Although bonds are typically issued with a variety of maturities, they can be categorized into one of three segments. These segments include short-term bonds, intermediate-term bonds, and long-term bonds. *Short-term* bonds have maturities of less than three years, *intermediate-term* bonds have maturities anywhere between four and nine years, and *long-term* bonds have maturities of ten years or longer. Long-term bonds tend to have higher yields than intermediate-term bonds, which tend to have higher yields than short-term bonds. Maturity segments will be discussed later in the chapter.

## Most Common Fixed-Income Types

- U.S. treasury notes and bonds
- State securities
- Municipal securities
- Government agency securities
- Corporate bonds

- Mortgage-backed securities
- Asset-backed securities
- Coins, bills, and related
- Bank holdings
- U.S. Treasury bills
- Money market funds
- Certificates of deposit

### Factors Influencing Fixed-Income Returns

- Macroeconomic forecasts
- Fiscal and monetary policies
- Rate of inflation (or deflation)
- Flow of funds
- Investors' behaviors, preferences, and risk tolerances
- Supply and demand for specific investments

## Positives and Negatives of Fixed-Income Investments

### Positives

- Low risk potential
- Tax advantages
- Low correlations to other asset classes
- Government securities (considered default-free)
- Priority of claims on assets
- Most current and predictable income
- Safety of principal
- Quick access to funds

### Negatives

- Low return potential
- Interest rate risk
- Prepayment risk
- Higher transaction costs
- Liquidity risk
- Greater price inefficiencies
- Purchasing power risk
- Reinvestment risk
- Small but existent default risk

# Historical Performance

Over time, long-term bonds have outperformed the other fixed-income types. Since holding longer-term bonds exposes you to greater levels of interest rate risk and increases the time you are exposed to credit and default risk, it is only appropriate that you should earn a higher return. Why else would you invest in a higher-risk asset unless you were properly compensated?

# Fixed-Income Volatility

The returns for long-term bonds are more volatile than both intermediate-term and short-term bonds. This is the result of greater risk inherent in longer-term bonds. Fortunately, holding higher-risk, more volatile long-term bonds pays off with higher returns over time. The same can be said for intermediate-term bonds over short-term bonds. This is an outstanding example of the golden rule of investing: risk and return are inescapably linked.

Not only are the returns of long-term bonds more volatile, but so too are their market prices. Market prices for fixed-income securities will fluctuate for any number of reasons. Some of these reasons include a change in market interest rates, strength or weakness of the macro economy, and security-specific risk unique to individual investments, namely credit and default risk.

There is a strong and positive correlation between length of maturity and volatility. The longer you hold an investment, the longer you are exposed to risk. The longer you are exposed to risk, the greater the probability that risk will turn into reality and misfortune will strike. Greater compensation in the form of higher return potential is then in order. For those with lower risk profiles either due to tolerance, capacity, or need, investing in shorter-term fixed-income investments is prudent. Unfortunately, lower risk potential is synonymous with lower return potential. Luckily, the decision on what level of risk to assume is entirely yours.

# Fixed-Income Correlations

Having a low correlation to equities is one of the greatest attributes of fixed-income investments. By combining fixed-income assets with an equity portfolio, you will enhance your portfolio's risk-adjusted return. Short-term bonds have the lowest correlations to equity assets. As the length of maturity increases, the correlation to equities also increases; however, the increase is only marginal.

Historically, short-term bonds have a correlation to equities of slightly less than zero. Intermediate-term bonds have a correlation of close to 0.1 whereas long-term bonds have a correlation of about 0.2 to equities. As you would anticipate, correlations to other fixed-income depend on the maturity. Short-term bonds have moderate to high correlations to intermediate-term bonds, which in turn have strong correlations to long-term bonds. The greatest differential is between short-term and long-term bonds.

These findings support adding fixed-income investments to a portfolio where diversification and enhancement to the risk-adjusted return are desired. The greatest benefit is provided when short-term bonds are added to an otherwise diversified multi-asset-class portfolio where equities comprise the backbone of the portfolio.

# Portfolio Enhancement Opportunities

Four opportunities for enhancing your portfolio's risk-and-return profile include *credit premium*, *tax-status premium*, *maturity premium*, and *high-yield premium*. Exercise care when pursuing any of these opportunities since they may be appropriate for some investors and not for others, given everyone's unique financial situation, goals, and needs. Also, always remember that although an asset class may exhibit high risk unique to itself, the synergistic benefits are what truly matter. It is the total portfolio that is important, not the constituent parts. We will begin with credit risk.

## Credit Premium

Credit risk refers to the uncertainty that a particular issuer will not make required interest payments. Companies with greater financial troubles are considered a greater credit risk than companies with a better financial picture. As an investor, you want to be compensated for taking on this extra risk. But how do you measure the credit risk of any particular company? You don't have to. There are three credit-rating agencies that most people have heard of. They include Standard & Poor's (S&P), Moody's, and Fitch. Each agency delves into the financials of most major publicly traded U.S. companies and issues a rating. All three credit-rating agencies have similar rating levels, but dissimilarities do exist. Ratings of BBB or better are considered investment-grade at both S&P and Fitch while a rating of Baa or higher at Moody's is considered investment-grade.

United States treasury and federal agency bonds have the least amount of credit risk and therefore receive the highest ratings. They typically yield the lowest as well. Risk and return are strongly linked. Municipalities and many corporations tend to receive the next highest ratings followed by questionable companies and even some municipalities. Bonds from these issuers are considered high-yield or junk bonds. These types of investments offer a unique premium and are discussed in more detail below.

The difference in bond ratings has a corresponding impact on the yield of bonds. Higher-rated bonds have lower yields and lower-rated bonds have higher yields. The variation in yields provides us with credit spreads. These spreads widen during periods of economic weakness and narrow during periods of economic strength. Research has shown that the average correlation between credit risk premiums and equity risk premiums is only about 25 percent. As a result, investing in bonds will enhance the risk-and-return profile of your portfolio. Bonds exhibiting greater credit risk provide excess return potential, but also have a slight increase in risk potential.

### *Tax-Status Premium*

Taxes often have the biggest impact on your portfolio returns. Their corrosive effect over time can be quite surprising. As a result, minimizing the impact of taxes should be a high priority. For some investors, investing in tax-exempt, or what are commonly called tax-free, bonds may be a smart and beneficial move. Investors with the highest total income tax rates will benefit the most from tax-exempt bonds. People with lower total income tax rates may be better off investing in taxable securities, paying the tax on any income or gain received, and still coming out ahead of what tax-exempt bonds provide.

In addition to your total income tax rate, the type of account you have will also play a role in determining whether or not taxable or tax-exempt investments make sense. For example, if you are investing in a tax-exempt account, investing in tax-free securities is not a wise move. Since you do not have to pay taxes on interest received from tax-free investments, they make more sense in taxable accounts. The same holds true for taxable securities. Their appeal is greater in tax-exempt accounts where taxes do not have to be paid on the current income received.

When comparing the yield on taxable bonds to the yield on tax-exempt bonds, multiply the taxable yield by your relevant total tax rate and subtract the result from that yield. For instance, if you were to buy a long-term corporate bond yielding 5 percent and your relevant total tax rate is 30 percent, then your after-tax return will be 3.5 percent. If the yield on a comparable, but tax-exempt, long-term municipal bond was 3.7 percent, then you would be wise to take advantage of the excess return by investing in the municipal bond. I used the word *relevant* since states will tax any income you receive from a bond issued by another state. I used the term *relevant total tax rate* since income from municipal bonds issued in your state of domicile is exempt from all federal, state, and local income taxes. Thus, you want to add your federal, state, and local income tax rates together to arrive at your total tax rate.

## Maturity Premium

Under normal economic conditions, bonds with longer maturities will pay higher yields than bonds with shorter maturities. This premium is the result of additional risk from an investor holding an investment where the principal is repaid much later. The longer an investment is held, the greater the interest rate risk, or risk that rising interest rates in the marketplace will create a lower demand for your lower-yielding bond. This lower demand will cause the price of your bond to fall in response. The longer the time to maturity, the greater the premium for holding that particular bond. Investors should receive a higher yield for bearing the higher risk. More risk potential equates to more return potential.

Duration is a mathematical concept in common practice in the investment field used to measure the price sensitivity of a bond to changing interest rates. Bonds with higher durations are more susceptible to changing interest rates and therefore change in market value more than bonds with lower durations. The length of maturity for a particular fixed-income security is the primary determinant of duration.

Fixed-income spreads, or the difference in yields, between shorter-term bonds and longer-term bonds can approach 1 percent and many times is even higher. During strong economic periods, the yield spread will increase as investors have more faith in the stability of higher-risk companies and their ability to pay interest and principal payments and therefore invest in them. In contrast, yield spreads typically narrow during periods of economic weakness as investors become skeptical of the prospects of riskier companies and therefore favor more secure companies, which issue correspondingly lower-yielding bonds. From a pure return standpoint, longer-term bonds may provide more benefit as they typically have higher yields. However, from a risk-adjusted standpoint, shorter-term bonds may be more ideal given their lower correlation to equity investments. The benefit of shorter-term bonds increases when portfolios have greater allocations to equities. A total bond index fund offers a quick, easy, and balanced solution.

## High-Yield Premium

Although frequently referred to as junk bonds, high-yield bonds play an important role in a properly allocated portfolio. High-yield bonds are speculative in nature, but when invested as a group, risk is controlled. High-yield bonds receive their earned title when one of the three credit-rating agencies assigns a *noninvestment-grade rating*. Earning this rating goes beyond simple credit risk. In question is the issuer's ability to not only make required interest payments but also to repay the principal at maturity. Given this added risk, commonly referred to as default risk, you should demand a higher return on your investment.

Default risk and equity risk are sometimes highly correlated, thus diminishing the benefits of allocating to both asset classes. However, the correlations frequently do fluctuate and even have become negative, which is an ideal situation. Research has demonstrated that the factors influencing equity and high-yield bond returns have little in common. This signals a fundamentally different asset class that is wise to consider for your portfolio. The most ideal method for investing in high-yield bonds is through a mutual fund. Given the high level of risk inherent in this asset class, investing in a professionally managed pool is best. Research has shown that although some issuers will default on their bonds, this impact is not great enough to offset the excess return you can capture by investing in a pool of high-yield bonds.

## Portfolio Allocation Considerations

An optimal portfolio emphasizes multiple asset classes with allocations to both equities and fixed income. Doing so will provide significant risk-and-return trade-off benefits, specifically the enhancement of total returns with only a moderate and manageable increase in portfolio risk. Fixed-income asset sub-classes include corporate bonds, high-yield bonds, government and agency bonds, cash and equivalents, mortgage-backed bonds, asset-backed bonds, and both developed and emerging market international bonds. The breadth and depth of fixed-income investing opportunities is significant. The potential is clearly available.

Your task is to evaluate your situation and determine what fixed-income allocation is most appropriate for you. Only you and your financial advisor are best positioned to accomplish this. The most ideal method for building an optimal portfolio with fixed-income investments is through a low-cost bond mutual fund, index fund, or exchange-traded fund. Although rather new to the investing scene, index funds and ETFs provide instant exposure to fixed-income and do so with only marginal cost. Moreover, index investments offer substantial diversification and efficient tax management. A total bond fund, such as the Lehman Aggregate Bond Fund, encompasses the majority of investment-grade fixed-income securities.

For those in the upper income tax brackets, municipal bonds should be considered in place of taxable corporate bonds. The net after-tax result could be higher.

| Index Fund | Symbol |
|---|---|
| iShares Lehman Aggregate Bond | AGG |
| Vanguard Total Bond Market | VBMFX |
| Vanguard High-Yield Corporate | VWEHX |
| TIAA-CREF High-Yield | TCHYX |
| iShares Lehman 1–3 Year Treasury | SHY |
| iShares Lehman 7–10 Year Treasury | IEF |
| iShares Lehman 20+ Year Treasury | TLT |
| iShares Lehman TIPS | TIP |
| Fidelity New Markets Income | FNMIX |
| Vanguard Limited-Term Tax-Exempt | VMLTX |

**Figure 6-1    Select Fixed-Income Investment Options**

## Select Investment Options

Figure 6-1 shows various investment options you may want to consider as you work at designing your optimal portfolio. Even though I support all index funds, I have only included low-cost and highly diversified index funds with an emphasis on exchange-traded funds. I strongly encourage you to evaluate the list in Figure 6-1 and determine for yourself if these investment options make sense for you. Depending on your financial situation and goals, you may want to incorporate a number of these or simply use one or two. The list is divided into multiple asset subclasses, with each group offering a different way to enhance the risk-adjusted return of your portfolio.

---

In the next chapter, you will learn about ways to amplify your portfolio by investing in alternative assets, such as commodities and real estate.

# 7

# Alternative Investments: Assets to Amplify Your Portfolio

## Overview of Alternative Assets

Alternative assets provide additional ways for you to maximize your portfolio's risk-adjusted return. This asset class goes beyond traditional equities and fixed-income investments. Your investing does not need to be limited to just stocks and bonds. This asset class has been gaining in popularity over the recent past with more and more investors allocating a portion of their portfolios to alternative assets.

Alternative assets comprise a very broad category of assets, mostly encompassing what are referred to as hard assets. In contrast to the other primary asset classes, alternative assets are more dissimilar in their inherent characteristics than they are similar. Furthermore, most alternative assets are tangible, rather than intangible as they are with the other primary asset classes. Alternative assets do well in times of high inflation, often capturing more

investment inflows during times of market weakness regardless of their perceived or intrinsic valuation.

One of the primary reasons underlying the purchase of alternative assets
is to protect purchasing power—a hedge against inflation. Another strong
reason investors should consider alternative assets is because they tend to
have very low, and sometimes negative, correlations with equities and bonds.
It is for these reasons that allocating alternative assets in your portfolio has
the potential to enhance return and reduce investment risk over time.

Although there are clear benefits to investing in alternative assets, there
are also a number of barriers and challenges to overcome. By far, the most
significant obstacle is total cost. Total cost includes purchase cost (commission
and bid-ask spread), management fees, and sales cost. As a result, you need to
fully investigate the potential benefits and evaluate them against the potential
costs. It is common to run into scenarios where the total costs far outweigh the
asset allocation benefits. Mutual funds and index investments provide the best
ways to gain exposure to this asset class and offer the easiest way to address
the challenges and hurdles with this asset class. Unfortunately, they often also
have high total cost hurdles that prove to be too high to overcome.

# Framework of Alternative Assets

The primary categories encompassed in this asset class include real estate;
private equities; commodities; foreign currencies; and collectibles such as artwork, rare stamps, and rare coins. There are many other categories such as
classic cars, vintage wines, and historic weapons that can be considered alternative assets. From a practicality standpoint, we will focus only on the primary
categories. Furthermore, although hedge funds themselves are not an asset
class, a brief discussion is provided since they offer the same benefits as do the
other alternative assets.

## Most Common Alternative Asset Types

- Real estate
- Commodities
- Private equity
- Hedge funds
- Collectibles

## Factors Influencing Alternative Asset Returns

There are several factors that influence the total returns of alternative assets. By
far, the largest factor is simple macro supply and demand. Supply is dictated

by pure availability of a certain asset, whereas demand is driven by perceived value. For this reason, many of the alternative asset classes are valued according to subjective value unique to individual investors. Collectibles are a prime example. One investor may place a significant value on an asset whereas another investor may not. A list of the primary factors influencing returns for asset allocation includes the following. Note that one factor may influence returns for one asset class, but not another.

- Supply and demand
- Flow of funds
- Rate of inflation or deflation
- Regulatory issues
- Currency exchange rates
- Transaction costs
- Management fees
- Shipping and holding costs

## Alternative Asset Subclasses

Given the vast dissimilarities among the different assets that comprise alternative assets, a breakout of each alternative asset subclass is necessary. No subclass has the same return potential or level of risk. Furthermore, the obstacles and costs of investing in them are also very different. The discussion of subclasses below begins with the most common asset subclass and concludes with the least common.

### Real Estate

*Real estate* is land, which includes the air above and the ground below, the permanent buildings or structures attached, and all the natural resources contained within the domain. Real estate is enticing as it has low correlations to both equities and fixed income. A properly allocated portfolio is allocated to real estate investments in addition to stocks and bonds. This combination of assets has proved to be one of the most effective ways of building a successful portfolio. Empirical research has shown that historical real estate returns have been comparable to equity returns. These returns, together with low equity correlations, are sufficient evidence for building a multi-asset-class portfolio that holds real estate.

Essentially you have two avenues to invest in real estate. First, you can buy real estate directly using funds from your investment portfolio or you can invest in real estate investment trusts (REITs). REITs are very similar to mutual funds in that you buy shares of a portfolio of real estate. They offer the most ideal way to gain immediate exposure to real estate in general. REITs are traded on U.S. stock exchanges similar to stock and are considered highly liquid, convenient, and usually well-diversified. Many REITs holdings include office buildings, apartments, malls, business centers, industrial buildings, and hotels. The total holdings still only account for less than 2 percent of the total stock market capitalization. The growth potential is thus very strong.

By directly investing in real estate, you gain total control over your investment. Decisions on leasing terms, amount to charge for rent, discretionary expenses to incur, and selling price are all at your discretion. However, directly owning real estate is not for everyone. Being actively involved in real estate is not for everyone. Many people have other responsibilities and would rather outsource the management to professionals. Another disadvantage is lack of real estate knowledge. This could prove to be disastrous.

For the vast majority of investors, passively investing in real estate is the preferred and best option. As a result, REITs are the ideal solution. The popularity of REITs has exploded over the last couple of decades due to tax law changes in the early 1990s. According to the National Association of Real Estate Investment Trusts (NAREIT), assets in REITs rose from $5.5 billion in 1990 to over $270 billion only 14 years later in 2004. At the same time, the number of REITs increased from 60 to 150. Furthermore, the total value of all REITs accounts for less than 10 percent of the total amount of investable U.S. real estate.

Under U.S. tax provisions, REITs must distribute at least 90 percent of their earnings to shareholders in the form of dividends or else be subject to corporate taxes. Consequently, most REITs abide by this provision. For investors, this means that the majority of their investment return is in the form of dividends rather than pure stock appreciation. The stock price of REITs typically advances with increases in the inflation rate since REITs income is principally derived from rents, which are tied to the inflation rate. In addition, rising inflation generally causes stock prices to fall; thus the simple flow of funds from stocks to real estate will drive REITs stock prices higher.

From a performance standpoint, REITs and stocks are very comparable. There have been periods when REITs have outperformed stocks and periods when stocks have outperformed REITs. However, in aggregate, the returns are very similar. Since the tax law changes affecting REITs in the early 1990s, the correlation between stocks and REITs has declined versus historical correlations. This equates to risk-and-return enhancement potential. Today, the correlation between the two is about 0.4 with a short-term ceiling of 0.5; thus, an opportunity for diversification is clearly evident.

To properly allocate your portfolio, real estate should be included. There are several low-cost REITs available from which to choose. A list of

| Index Fund | Symbol |
|---|---|
| Cohen & Steers Realty Majors | ICF |
| iShares Dow Jones U.S. Real Estate | IYR |
| Vanguard REIT | VGSIX |
| iShares Goldman Sachs Natural Resources | IGE |
| iShares Dow Jones U.S. Energy Sector | IYE |
| iShares S&P Global Energy Sector | IXC |
| Vanguard Energy | VGENX |
| iShares Dow Jones U.S. Basic Materials | IYM |
| iShares COMEX Gold Trust | IAU |
| Vanguard Precious Metals Mining | VGMPX |
| Oppenheimer Real Asset | QRAAX |

**Figure 7-1    Select Alternative Investment Options**

potential investments is provided in Figure 7-1. I highly suggest you consider one of them for your real estate asset class.

## Positives of Real Estate

- Significant tax advantages
- Low correlations to the other asset classes
- High current income potential

## Negatives of Real Estate

- High transaction costs
- Greater market inefficiencies
- Liquidity concerns

## Commodities

Dating back even longer than equities and fixed income, *commodities* are tangible articles of trade that are indistinguishable and thus interchangeable with each other. They can be processed and resold and often have other substitutes within the same asset class. Uniformity is the universal theme. Commodities are common articles a person may use, either directly or indirectly, on a daily basis. Specifically, these articles include agricultural products such as orange juice, sugar, soy, wheat, and corn; precious metals such as gold and silver; basic materials such as copper, nickel, and steel; and energy products such as power, crude oil, natural gas, and coal.

The market for commodities is truly global. There is no limitation on supply and demand for most commodities. Any shortage is followed by efforts to build up the supply of that commodity by suppliers. Demand for commodities can be met on a global scale as well. Regardless of where you are located, purchasing or selling a commodity is relatively quick and easy.

The advantage of commodities is that they exhibit a low correlation to both equities and bonds. Consequently, when the stock market is experiencing weakness, commodities are relatively stable and hold their own. Unfortunately, commodity returns have been low historically. This is particularly bad given the obstacles. The benefit of owning commodities may therefore not be worth the costs. Worse yet, commodity prices are volatile, thus there is more risk. This translates to a situation where you assume more risk than appropriate for a historically low return—not the most desirable investment scenario.

## Positives of Commodities

- Hedge against inflation
- Low correlations to other asset classes
- Ability to leverage purchase

## Negatives of Commodities

- Historically low returns
- Greatly impacted by geopolitical events
- Highly volatile prices

## Private Equity

Sometimes referred to as private investments, *private equity* is a very broad term that actually refers to any form of equity investments in companies that are not freely traded, nor listed on public stock exchanges. The companies invested in are private companies. Some of the primary types of private equity include venture capital (VC), mezzanine capital, leveraged buyouts (LBOs), managed buyouts (MBOs), fund of funds, growth capital, and angel investing. These companies are generally illiquid and thought of as long-term investments. Many target investments are new companies that offer high return but high risk potential. Taking these companies public through an Initial Public Offering (IPO) is the overall goal. At the same time, many other target companies are more mature where buyouts are used to take them private with the hope of taking them public again some time later and making a hefty profit for doing so.

There are typically a number of restrictions on the transfer of ownership, but private equity investments are not subject to the same high level of government oversight and regulation as are publicly traded companies.

Private equities are generally organized as partnerships when there is one or more general partners and numerous limited partners. Once a particular partnership has reached its target size, the partnership is closed to new investors, including new funds from existing investors. Since the early 1990s, private equities have experienced massive growth with solid year after year rising of capital growth rates. The allure of private equities is tempting; however, remember the high-risk potential and the barriers to acquisition and liquidation. This alternative asset class is surely not for everyone, but some investors may find it quite beneficial.

## Positives of Private Equities

- Significant return potential
- Low correlations to the other asset classes
- Ability to focus investments to desired industry segments

## Negatives of Private Equities

- Substantial risk
- Regulatory concern
- Marginal liquidity

## Hedge Funds

*Hedge funds* are lightly regulated private investment pools managed for ultra affluent investors where investments are characterized by unconventional strategies. These strategies typically employ moderate to aggressive investing, although some hedge funds are considered conservative. Some of the more speculative strategies include selling short; using significant leverage; employing computer program trading; and incorporating derivatives such as options, swaps, and futures. By law, hedge funds are restricted to a low and limited number of accredited investors and are primarily organized as limited partnerships. As a result, the vast majority of hedge funds target institutions and wealthy individuals. The term hedge fund dates back to Alfred Winslow Jones who in 1949 started the first hedge fund by selling short stocks.

As mentioned previously, a hedge fund is not a true alternative asset class. However, given the benefits and characteristics of hedge funds, a mention of them under alternative assets is appropriate. Hedge funds are pooled investment vehicles that are managed by professional money managers. Thus, the concept of hedge funds is quite similar to mutual funds. The difference for practical investment purposes is *how* they invest and *what* they invest in. Other differences include management disclosures, fees, and government restrictions on the number of investment participants. The lack of regulatory oversight provides hedge fund managers with significant flexibility in taking investment action and in investment options. This can be both a golden opportunity or a hidden risk. For this reason, if mutual funds are considered buses and minivans, then hedge funds are considered shinning, sleek, and sought after sports cars. There are more than 8,000 hedge funds today, but close to 12 percent close every year.

Many styles of hedge funds have low correlations to both equities and fixed-income, thus making them attractive options for enhancing your portfolio. Unfortunately, many hedge funds have excessive management fees, with the average around 1.4 percent annually. Many hedge funds also take 20 percent of any gains they make for their investors. This is good and bad. Good because it gives the hedge fund managers an incentive to deliver strong results, but bad since it not only pains investors to give away such a large portion of earnings but also because it gives hedge fund managers extra motivation to take higher risks. Investors know this going in, so the problem is mitigated. For more on hedge funds, please read *Understanding Hedge Funds* (Scott Frush and McGraw-Hill).

## Positives of Hedge Funds

- High return potential
- Low correlations to the other asset classes
- Multiple styles for different investors
- Ability to earn positive returns in both bull and bear markets

## Negatives of Hedge Funds

- High management fees, including performance fees
- Large initial investment
- Typically higher risk
- Tax concerns
- Limited liquidity and locks on withdrawing funds

## *Collectibles*

Collectibles are assets such as paintings, sculptures, fine artwork, rare coins and stamps, plus nearly any other valuable asset that can be collected and traded. Collectibles are essentially creative objects that can be purchased and sold by a willing buyer and seller for reasons other than their aesthetic beauty. As you know, you cannot hold art in your portfolio as you can with real estate and commodities. However, collectibles can be purchased with funds that would otherwise be earmarked for your portfolio.

The primary disadvantage of collectibles is the acquisition cost and storage cost. Insurance premiums can also be a burden. These costs will reduce total performance making them less attractive as an investment option. Other disadvantages include a lack of liquidity and lack of expertise in buying and valuing the collectibles. However, both financial return and aesthetic benefits can offset these disadvantages.

### *Positives of Collectibles*

- Aesthetic gratification
- Low risk
- Multiple styles for different investors
- Low correlations with other asset classes

### *Negatives of Collectibles*

- Cost of acquisition, storage, and insurance
- Inefficient and illiquid market
- Different investor preferences
- Lack of buying and valuing expertise

## Alternative Asset Volatility and Correlations

One of the primary reasons for investing in alternative assets is their low correlations with both equities and fixed-income assets. This provides you with opportunities for enhancing the risk-adjusted return of your portfolio. During periods of equity or fixed-income decline, many commodities will remain unaffected. Thus, for investors looking to better manage their investment risk, commodities offer a means to do so. However, this comes with a cost, and that is potentially higher volatility and historically lower returns for some asset types. For example, commodity prices have been highly volatile historically. Furthermore, the return earned during the same time period has not been much better than the rates an investor could have earned on treasury investments. Fortunately, assets such as real estate offer a solid way for you to earn nice returns and provide for risk reduction through a low correlation to equity assets.

## Portfolio Allocation Considerations

Asset classes represent building blocks for the selection of appropriate invest-ments and determination of an optimal asset allocation. As a result, under-standing each alternative asset class, its expected risk-and-return trade-off profile, and the correlations to each asset class is therefore essential.

Given the different alternative asset classes available, you can customize your portfolio in a way most suitable for achieving your objectives and constraints. You must use each asset class in order to enhance your portfolio's return while reducing its risk. Some alternative asset classes are excellent ways to amplify your portfolio, such as real estate, while others only offer limited returns with disproportionately higher risk. Care, skill, and patience are needed to evaluate each asset class and decide how each one will enhance your overall portfolio.

The costs of some alternative asset classes are simply too high to over-come. Excessive costs have the potential of outweighing the benefit you can earn from allocating a portion of your portfolio to them. If you feel com-pelled to invest in alternative assets, index investments are the best approach. Immediate asset class exposure, significant diversification, tax-efficiency, and low costs make them hard to pass up. At this time, there are only a limited number of index funds targeting alternative assets. However, you can be sure that you will see more investment companies offering additional alternative asset index funds over time as their popularity increases.

## Select Investment Options

Figure 7-1 is a list of alternative asset index investments you may want to consider for your own portfolio. Investigate them fully before investing to ensure they are not only appropriate for you but also will help you achieve your financial goals and needs. The list is divided into multiple asset sub-classes for ease in identifying specific investable asset subclasses.

---

In the next chapter, you will learn about global asset allocation and how it can take your portfolio on a trip to greener pastures.

# 8

# Global Investments: Assets without Borders

## Importance of Global Asset Allocation

Global financial markets have experienced dynamic changes over the last couple of decades. U.S. equities now account for less than half of the total global equity market capitalization. This figure is down from more than two-thirds just a couple of decades ago. As a result, investors who incorporate international assets into their portfolios will find greater opportunities to protect and grow their investments. More specifically, they will improve the risk-and-return trade-off profile inherent in their portfolio by adding international assets to their asset mix. Consider, for example, two football teams, one with 45 players and one with 100 players. Since only 11 players are on the field at any one particular time, the chance of the team with 100 players finding better players is higher than the team with 45 players. Of course this is not the case in all situations, but it is for the vast majority. It is simply the law of numbers. By the way, the numbers 45 and 100 were not selected at random. The 45 is the approximate percentage of the global equity market that the U.S. market represented in the mid 1990s, whereas the 100 simply represents the entire global equity market (100 percent).

Historically, most individual investors did not pay attention to investing globally for three principal reasons:

- Investors did not realize the benefits.
- Transaction costs were substantial.
- Information for making investment decisions was unreliable or, worse yet, absent.

Over the years, both transactions costs and availability of information have become more favorable, and many investors have realized the benefits of adding international investments to their portfolios. According to the International Monetary Fund (IMF), U.S. households have increased their percentage of foreign assets from 1.8 percent in the period 1986–1990 to 6.6 percent in the period 1996–1999 (*World Economic Outlook*, October 2001, p. 75).

Adding international assets to an investment portfolio does not come without risk. There are new and different risks confronting the global investor. In addition, some risks that a U.S. investor faces are significantly magnified in foreign markets. For example, market liquidity is not as robust in most foreign countries as it is in the United States. Even so, adding international assets to an investment portfolio still has more potential rewards than potential risks.

## Benefits of Global Asset Allocation

The ability of investors to reduce portfolio risk is limited in portfolios comprised of purely U.S. assets. Investors are able to reduce total risk by minimizing investment-specific risk. However, investors cannot reduce systematic risk, or risk attributed to the market and other uncontrollable external factors. That brings up a good question. What is the market? The market we have been talking about is the U.S. market. However, when investors add international assets to their portfolios, the market portfolio changes to encompass both the U.S. market and the foreign market from where the assets are added. Thus, reducing market risk is at the heart of global asset allocation.

The reduction of total risk from global asset allocation is driven by the less than perfect correlations between U.S. assets and international assets. As we discussed in Chapter 3, we know that asset classes that are not perfectly, positively correlated with each other will provide return-enhancing and risk-reducing benefits to your portfolio.

Global correlations are different from country to country, some highly correlated to the United States and some not. More highly developed countries tend to have higher correlations with that of the United States and other developed countries due in large part to the significant degree of economic interaction. The more interaction among countries, the more influence each country has on the economic conditions of all the others. Conversely, the less interaction countries have with another, the more insulated they are from each other's economic influences, both positive and negative.

The greatest benefits from adding international assets to a portfolio come from those countries that have the lowest correlations to the United States. However, the governments of many less-developed countries often place harsh regulations and severe restrictions on the investments and withdrawals of funds from their countries. Higher potential returns come with higher potential risks.

# Methods to Invest Globally

There are a number of methods you can use to add international assets to your portfolio. Some are quite effective whereas a couple offer only minor benefits.

## Direct Investments

Direct investments allow you to purchase assets via a foreign exchange, such as the London Stock Exchange or the Tokyo Stock Exchange. Unfortunately, there are a number of disadvantages to this method. First, it is significantly more difficult to obtain information on industries and companies in many foreign countries. Second, you generally face new and problematic investment regulations and restrictions unique to each country. You will learn about global asset allocation and how it can take your portfolio on a trip to greener pastures. Third, transaction costs (commissions and bid-ask spreads) associated with trading on foreign exchanges are usually higher, thus eroding the net return of an investment. Fourth, evaluating foreign assets for investment is challenging using U.S. analytical techniques. For example, different countries have different rules for what constitutes net income. Some countries allow certain accounting practices while others do not. As a result, earnings per share data from country to country are often not comparable. Thus, using the same analytical techniques is not always appropriate. Lastly, simply exchanging currency can be quite challenging.

## U.S. Listed Foreign Investments

This method can be summarized as "invest globally by investing locally." Instead of purchasing foreign assets via a foreign exchange, you purchase foreign assets directly on the New York Stock Exchange (NYSE) or the American Stock Exchange (Amex). Shares of foreign companies such as Sony and Daimler-Chrysler are listed and traded on U.S. exchanges as well as on their home exchanges.

Purchasing foreign investments on a U.S. exchange has some advantages over purchasing them on a foreign exchange: you do not have to deal with a currency exchange and investment information is readily available. To be listed on the NYSE, the U.S. Securities and Exchange Commission requires foreign companies to conform to U.S. Generally Accepted Accounting Principles, or what is commonly referred to as GAAP. As a result, you are able to make much better evaluations and investment decisions. The major downside to this method is that most foreign companies do not list on a U.S. exchange, giving you a narrow list of investment options.

## International Mutual Funds

International mutual funds are essentially the same as U.S. mutual funds in that they each comprise a pool of investments and are managed by a professional portfolio manager. The simple difference is that international mutual funds comprise international assets rather than U.S. assets. The concept of the international mutual fund has been around for quite some time. As a matter of fact, one of the very first hybrid international mutual funds was established back in the late 1700s in Holland. The fund was comprised of Russian and Mecklenburg government bonds, Bank of Vienna fixed-income securities, loans from the Spanish canal, English colonial securities, loans from South American plantations, and debt instruments from assorted Danish-American endeavors.

One advantage of international mutual funds is their specialized professional management. In addition, as with most mutual funds, international mutual funds offer immediate diversification and substantial liquidity to investors. International mutual funds allow you to build a portfolio with a relatively small investment. Finally, international mutual funds are denominated in U.S. dollars, thus eliminating the need and hassle of exchanging currency.

There are two primary disadvantages of international mutual funds. First, most target certain geographic regions of the globe. Consequently, your risk-and-return trade-off benefits may be constrained. Investing in a group of international mutual funds where each target different regions of the globe can help overcome this problem. Second and most important, international mutual funds often have very high expenses and management fees, sometimes approaching 2 percent annually. This of course is in direct response to the specialized research and operating expenditures that are required to operate the fund.

## International Closed-End Funds

Closed-end funds are similar to mutual funds in that they represent a pool of investments managed by a professional portfolio manager. In contrast, international closed-end funds are listed on U.S. exchanges and have a fixed number of shares outstanding. This particular characteristic is an advantage of international closed-end funds. As a result, portfolio managers do not need to keep cash on hand to meet shareholder withdrawals, which allows the fund to be fully invested at all times. In addition, during periods of market weakness, portfolio managers are not forced to sell investments to meet shareholder withdrawals. Eliminating the need to invest new money or to liquidate existing investments to meet shareholder withdrawals is advantageous, especially with international closed-end funds that target less liquid and less-developed countries.

Prices for international closed-end funds are determined entirely by market demand. As a result, international closed-end funds can trade at either a discount or a premium to the market value of their holdings (often referred to as *net asset value* or NAV). Buying an international closed-end fund then becomes more complex and requires greater analysis. However, investors can use the premium or discount to their advantage. For example, let's say there is a market crash in German equities. International closed-end funds targeting this region will see their net asset values decline proportionally to the loss in German equities. Now say equities in this region begin to rally, but investors remain cautious leading to lower demand for these closed-end funds than for the equities these funds hold. Over time, investors' interests increase and they begin to make purchases, resulting in shrinking discounts. Those investors who took advantage of the rally in German equities by purchasing a closed-end fund will have experienced a double benefit of rising NAVs and shrinking discounts. Today, many international closed-end funds trade with large discounts, sometimes as high as 20 percent. In addition, it is not surprising to see premiums and discounts last for a number of years.

Now that we have discussed the advantages of international closed-end funds, let's shift gears and quickly discuss the principal disadvantage. Most international closed-end funds are highly targeted investments, usually focusing on only one particular country or region. As a result, international closed-end funds do not provide a good method to add international assets to your investment portfolio. You would need to add a significant number of international closed-end funds representing different countries in order to achieve proper global asset allocation.

## Stocks of Global Mega-Corporations

This method simply involves purchasing securities of U.S. global corporations without directly purchasing foreign securities. Since U.S. global corporations have operations across the globe, they will be impacted by each country in which they operate. For example, if a corporation has a factory in country A and riots in that country cause a shutdown in operations, then the corporation will be impacted by a loss of revenue. This in turn will decrease corporate earnings to some degree. In theory, this method appears sound. However, studies have shown that the stocks of U.S. global corporations trade very similarly to U.S. nonglobal corporations. Consequently, this method provides little in the way of benefits from global asset allocation.

## American Depository Receipts

American Depository Receipts (ADRs) are stocks issued in the United States by large U.S. money center banks. Each ADR represents an ownership interest in a fixed number of shares of a foreign company. The major advantage of ADRs is that they trade either on a U.S. exchange or over-the-counter, depending on whether or not the foreign company is registered with the SEC. As a result, ADRs are denominated in U.S. dollars, thus eliminating the need to exchange currency. They can be bought and sold like U.S. stocks and their dividends are paid in U.S. dollars.

Being listed on a U.S. exchange allows an investor to trade the security and have the transaction completed much quicker. Unlike direct purchases on foreign exchanges, ADRs settle just as quickly and easily as U.S. stocks do. Thus, investors encounter fewer operational problems than do investors who purchase foreign securities directly.

Today there are more than 1,500 ADRs available for investment in the United States. Although ADRs have been in use since the 1920s, they have become increasingly more popular in recent years. The popularity of ADRs is primarily due to the greater interest and participation from foreign companies who view ADRs as a way to raise needed capital, increase and diversify their base of shareholders, and create and enhance support for their goods and services in the U.S. marketplace.

Although ADRs are traded in U.S. dollars, their prices are indirectly influenced by currency exchange fluctuations. In general, the stronger the performance of the U.S. dollar versus a foreign currency, the worse the net investment return. In contrast, the weaker the performance of the U.S. dollar versus a foreign currency, the better the net investment return. Moreover, it is extremely difficult to forecast future exchange rates, thus leaving investors at the mercy of macroeconomic factors.

A disadvantage of ADRs is that some foreign corporations do not adhere to U.S. GAAP. This problem creates more challenging evaluations and investment decision making. Another disadvantage is that not all foreign corporations have underlying ADRs. Therefore, investors have fewer investment alternatives with this method.

Given the current trend toward increased globalization, the future for ADRs is murky at best. Why? The reason is because other methods of investing internationally will probably become more preferred. For example, the number of foreign stocks listed on U.S. exchanges will undoubtedly increase over time. Since money center banks will be out of the picture, transaction costs will decline. In addition, the quantity and quality of information on foreign companies will increase, allowing for more informed evaluations and better investment decisions.

### International Index Investments

International index investments may provide the best method for you to achieve global asset allocation. International index investments provide broad market exposure and high degrees of diversification at very low costs. International index investments trade on U.S. exchanges in about the same way as do shares of U.S. publicly traded companies. However, international index investments are not shares of a company. Rather, they are shares of a portfolio designed to closely track the performance of any number of market indices. Each international index investment closely tracks a specific market, offering an effective method to obtain cost-effective exposure to the markets and sectors desired.

## Global Asset Allocation Risks

In aggregate, international investments generally offer higher return potential than U.S. investments. However, you should keep in mind that investing internationally typically involves increased risk. Nonetheless, international investments are still ideal since they are not perfectly, positively correlated with U.S. investments and thus provide return-enhancing and risk-reducing benefits to your portfolio. International investments tend to be more risky than U.S. investments for the following reasons.

### Currency Fluctuation

Exchange rates between the U.S. dollar and foreign currencies are constantly changing due to supply and demand for each currency. As a result, currency exchange rates can substantially increase or decrease the net return (expressed in U.S. dollars) of your investment made abroad even if the market value of your investment did not change during the holding period.

EXAMPLE: A U.S. real estate investment group purchases a commercial property in Canada for $500,000 Canadian. If one year later the value of the property remains at $500,000 Canadian and the Canadian dollar has declined in value versus the U.S. dollar, then the U.S. real estate investment group will experience a negative holding period return. Why? Because if the U.S. real estate investment group were to sell the property, it would take more depreciated Canadian dollars to buy appreciated U.S. dollars.

## Political Risk

Political risk refers to the uncertainty that political decisions, policies, events, and conditions in a foreign country will adversely impact the values of investments made in that particular country. Political risk takes many forms such as trade agreements, severe tariffs, interference with operations, confiscation of property, economic instability, repatriation of profits, restrictions, war, revolution, terrorism and sabotage, kidnap and ransom, extortion, and lack of, or reliability of, financial information.

## Lack of Liquidity

You may find it challenging to trade securities in less-developed countries due to their smaller market size and resulting lower inherent supply and demand. In fact, at times there may be little to no demand for an investment that you need to sell. As a result, you may be forced to liquidate your investment at a much lower price than expected, even if detrimental to your net investment return.

## Merging of Asset Correlations

Over time, as global economies progressively become more integrated, so too do correlations among countries. This development is slow, but steady. Today, nearly 50 percent of the global market capitalization and 40 percent of global sales are attributed to multinational corporations. This trend will only become more pronounced as global corporations increase their global operations either through organic growth or through the acquisition of foreign companies. As a result of the rising correlations, the risk-and-return trade-off benefits from global asset allocation will lessen. However, as we have discussed previously, as long as correlations are not perfect, there is opportunity for you to enhance your returns while reducing your risk.

# Your Allocation to Global Assets

There is a significant debate as to how much you should allocate to international assets. The best answer is to base the allocation on your risk tolerance.

For those investors who aspire for a higher return and are willing and able to assume a higher risk, they can allocate a substantial portion of their portfolio to international assets, possibly close to 50 percent. Conversely, for those investors who have lower risk tolerances and lower return aspirations, they can allocate a much smaller portion, if any, of their portfolio to international assets, possibly anywhere from 5 to 15 percent.

Given the risks of investing globally, adding international assets to an investment portfolio requires greater analysis and evaluation. Although you may have the ability to perform these tasks, you may still want to seek professional advice.

## Investment Options

The following chart provides some investment options you may want to consider for your own portfolio. As a strong proponent of index funds, I have only included low-cost and highly-diversified index funds with an emphasis to exchange-traded funds. I strongly encourage you to evaluate the list below and determine for yourself if these investment options make sense for your needs. Depending on your financial situation and goals, you may want to incorporate a number of these or simply use one or two. The chart is divided into multiple asset subclasses, each offering portfolio risk/return enhancement opportunities.

| Index Fund | Symbol |
| --- | --- |
| iShares MSCI EAFE | EFA |
| iShares S&P Global 100 | IOO |
| StreetTRACKS DJ Global Titans | DGT |
| Fidelity Spartan International | FSIIX |
| Vanguard Developed Markets | VDMIX |
| Vanguard Emerging Markets Stock | VEIEX |
| Vanguard Total International Stock | VGTSX |
| Vanguard European Stock | VEURX |
| Vanguard Pacific Stock | VPACX |
| iShares MSCI Emerging Markets | EEM |

Figure 8-1   Select Global Investment Options

# PART THREE

# DETERMINING AND MANAGING YOUR ASSET ALLOCATION

# 9

CHAPTER

# Multi-Asset-Class Portfolios: Behavior and Selection Framework

## Asset Class Behavior

At certain time periods, certain asset classes will perform well, whereas during other time periods, other asset classes will perform well. Unfortunately, we do not know which asset class will perform well during any specific period, and therefore it is vitally important to be invested in multiple asset classes at all times. The benefit of multi-asset-class investing is the reduction of portfolio investment risk and the increase in portfolio investment return potential. This is the essence of a true lower-risk, higher-return portfolio.

> Let every man divide his money into three parts, and invest a third in land, a third in business, and a third let him keep in reserve.
>
> —*Talmud axiom*
> *Circa 1200 B.C.–A.D. 500*

You receive diversification and allocation benefits when you invest in multiple asset classes that have fundamental differences among them. The principal benefit is to enhance the risk-adjusted return of your portfolio. This is referred to as the *allocation effect*. However, allocating to multiple asset classes does not guarantee consistently higher returns with corresponding low risk. That simply cannot be accomplished consistently over time. During certain periods of time your portfolio will experience strong asset allocation benefits, whereas during other times your portfolio will experience weak asset allocation benefits.

A well-constructed portfolio will not behave in a fashion that projects the sum of its parts—its asset classes. Rather, a portfolio will behave in a fashion that projects the sum of its synergies. Asset class synergies are created by the interaction of the asset classes comprising a portfolio. The interaction between asset classes is commonly referred to as correlation and is a critical input to the asset allocation process. Correlation is the mathematical measurement used to describe how closely the market prices of two assets move together. Positively correlated asset classes move in the same direction, both up and down, whereas negatively correlated asset classes move in opposite directions. Correlations between two assets are expressed on a scale between $-1.0$ and $+1.0$ where $+1.0$ is considered perfectly, positively correlated and $-1.0$ is perfectly, negatively correlated.

By investing in asset classes that possess low to negative correlations, you reduce total portfolio risk without impacting portfolio return. In theory, you should allocate to asset classes that are perfectly, negatively correlated. However, in the real world there are no asset classes that are perfectly, negatively correlated. In reality, most asset classes are positively correlated to some degree. Regardless of the positive correlation, holding two or more asset classes will reduce volatility risk below the weighted average of the individual volatility risks. The behavior of a multi-asset-class portfolio is therefore different from the constituent investments evaluated alone.

Asset class correlations will not remain static over time; they will change with the changing marketplace. Correlations tend to rise when the market is advancing and fall when the market is declining. Furthermore, research has shown that correlations fall quicker than they rise. This is a good thing since lower correlations are better.

Under asset allocation, the expected return of a portfolio is simply the weighted average of the expected returns of the asset classes within a portfolio. Regardless of the degree of volatility, expected return will remain constant. On the other hand, volatility risk will not remain constant as the synergies of holding multiple asset classes will lessen the overall risk, even below the average risk level. This is a clear example of the benefit of multi-asset-class investing.

A portfolio comprising only two asset classes has fewer benefits than that of a portfolio with three or more asset classes. The more asset classes that are included, the more ideal the risk-adjusted return becomes. Minimizing portfolio risk for a given level of return is considered an efficient portfolio. As a result, it is common sense to allocate to multiple asset classes and diversify where needed. Although it is not always wise to allocate to all available asset classes in the marketplace, keep in mind that more asset classes are typically preferable.

In contrast to asset allocation, diversification is not underscored by the trade-off between risk and return. Rather, it is underscored by the idea that as you add more investments with essentially the same risk-and-return trade-off profile, in regard to investment-specific risk, the less each investment will impact the overall portfolio. The goal of diversification is to minimize investment-specific risk, thus leaving a portfolio with only market risk. To gain the greatest diversification benefits, only those investments with relatively the same risk-and-return trade-off profiles should be purchased or else the overall portfolio risk-and-return trade-off profile will change.

The benefits of asset allocation are quite powerful in terms of both risk reduction and return enhancement. Different asset classes have different levels of risk and return that tend to differ from other asset classes. All else being equal, asset classes with lower correlations make ideal candidates for portfolio allocation. Fundamentally different asset classes are key to gaining asset allocation benefits. Locating asset classes that fit this mold is a cumbersome project. Fortunately, the global marketplace offers numerous asset classes with varying styles, sizes, and fundamentals. With the United States holding less than 50 percent of the investable securities in the world, alternatives abound for asset allocation opportunities. Patience, discipline, and effort will go a long way to locating suitable asset classes.

In order to determine your optimal asset allocation comprising multiple asset classes you must have a solid understanding of some very important points. First, there is no perfect allocation or perfect plan. There are only good to very good plans that will help you achieve your goals. Second, make sure to learn the key specifics of each asset class, such as general correlations, historical returns, and common risk levels. Third, understand that forecasting future correlations, returns, risk levels, and price movements is an extremely difficult endeavor. Don't waste your time. Fourth, a multi-asset-class portfolio is more ideal than a portfolio with only one asset class. More is typically better. Lastly, remember to build a portfolio with an asset allocation that addresses your financial goals, objectives, and constraints. One portfolio allocation is not ideal for everyone, thus selecting an asset allocation can be more of an art than a science.

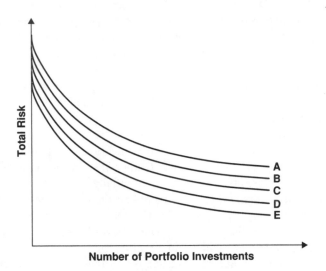

**Figure 9-1    Advantage of Multi-Asset-Class Portfolios**
        **(A) Portfolio of large-cap stocks**
        **(B) Portfolio of large-cap stocks *and* small-cap value stocks**
        **(C) Portfolio of large-cap stocks, small-cap value stocks, *and* corporate bonds**
        **(D) Portfolio of large-cap stocks, small-cap value stocks, corporate bonds, *and* real estate**
        **(E) Portfolio of large-cap stocks, small-cap value stocks, corporate bonds, real estate, *and* international stocks**

## Asset Class Selection

The selection of asset classes is a process based exclusively on a number of very important factors, or portfolio allocation inputs as I call them. These factors can be classified as either *investor-centric* inputs or *investment-centric* inputs. The investor-centric inputs are based on your own attitudes and investment-related objectives and constraints. For example, some investors desire a higher return and have a greater risk capacity than other investors. As a result, their portfolio allocation will differ from less aggressive investors, and sometimes in a profound way. Investment-centric inputs, on the other hand, are not directly related to the investor but arise directly from the market. For instance, investments with higher volatilities have greater risk and therefore impact how you determine your asset allocation. A second investment-centric input is correlation, the lower the better.

    An important first step is to fully identify what you are looking to achieve; namely, what are your return aspirations? What is your risk profile and what are your unique constraints that influence the asset mix of your portfolio? Below is a discussion of the portfolio allocation inputs, divided into the investor-centric inputs and the investment-centric inputs.

# Investor-Centric Inputs

## SMART Goals

Having investment goals and striving to attain those goals will give your investing purpose. With asset allocation, goals will directly impact your asset allocation. Do you need money in one year for a new home or will you be receiving a lump sum retirement distribution? As a result, you may want to allocate a greater amount to fixed-income and a correspondingly lower allocation to equities. As mentioned in Chapter 3, matching asset classes to goals is key to building your optimal portfolio. SMART illustrates the five characteristics of well-designed goals.

- Specific: Your goals should be unambiguous, clear, and well-defined.
- Measurable: Your goals should be quantifiable and calculable.
- Accepted: Your goals should be acknowledged and motivational.
- Realistic: Your goals should be achievable and attainable, not lofty.
- Time-centric: Your goals should be for a set period, nothing indefinite.

## Investment Knowledge

Time and time again we hear "invest in what you know." Both Warren Buffet and Peter Lynch propagated this belief. The more knowledgeable you are about a specific investment, the more confident you are that the investment is appropriate and suitable. On the flip side, the less you know about an investment, the more apprehensive and uncertain you are about whether or not to hold that particular investment in your portfolio.

All else being equal, the greater an investor's investment knowledge, the higher his or her risk tolerance tends to be. An investor with strong investment knowledge will typically have a portfolio with higher risk investments, while an investor with weaker investment knowledge will tend to design a portfolio with lower to moderate investment holdings.

## Investment Objectives

The most common investment objectives that investors tend to have is to protect their portfolios and to grow them the right way over time. In other words, they want to earn a sufficient return. Return aspiration is the desired financial reward sought by all investors for deferring current consumption and making an investment. The reward for making an investment can come in two forms: appreciation of principal and receipt of dividends and interest income.

As an investor you need to gain a better perspective on what return it is going to take in order to achieve your SMART goals. For example, you may need a slightly higher return to build a portfolio large enough to fund your retirement sometime in the future. Other quantifiable goals may include needing $25,000 per year for college tuition beginning in five years or needing $100,000 to start your own business. Lastly, your return aspiration should be realistic, neither vague nor unattainable.

## Current and Projected Financial Position

Your level of wealth will play a big role in determining your asset alloca-
tion. In general, investors with higher levels of wealth tend to have greater capacity for assuming risk. Simply put, wealthy investors have more room for error in achieving their goals. Of course this is not always the case, but as a general rule it usually holds true. For instance, if you were to win the lottery, your capacity to assume risk would increase dramatically. Wouldn't you care less about losing $50,000 if you just won $25,000,000?

## Risk Profile

Your risk profile is perhaps the most important input to the portfolio man-
agement process. Your risk profile will not only determine how you allocate your portfolio from the outset but also how you manage your portfolio over time. Your risk profile is comprised of three similar, yet still separate, fac-
tors. These include your *tolerance* for risk, your *capacity* to assume risk, and your *need* to assume risk. The lowest value in any one of the three factors is considered the maximum level of risk you should assume in your portfolio. For example, although an investor may have a high-risk tolerance and high capacity to assume risk, that investor may not have the need to assume risk. Why? The reason is because many investors do not have the need to assume risk since their wealth is more than adequate to fund their lifestyle and goals, now and in the future. Unfortunately, investor risk profile is difficult to measure for three reasons. First, risk is specific to individual situations. Second, risk is not easily understood, and people therefore act irrationally and without predictability. Third, investor risk tolerance, risk capacity, and need for risk change over time; they are not static. Thus, your risk profile could always be moving and not easy to isolate.

Since you cannot control investment results, risk tolerance is therefore based on your tolerance for volatility. Investments with greater volatility have higher chances of experiencing price declines, which means you may not achieve your return aspiration.

Determining your risk tolerance is rather subjective and therefore difficult to express as a variable. One good solution to determining your risk tolerance is to complete a risk tolerance questionnaire. Most financial services firms offer them to their investors. However, note that risk tolerance questionnaires have two flaws. First, they often try to measure your risk tolerance, risk capacity, and risk need all at the same time. Three different questionnaires with a face-to-face follow-up discovery meeting should then be used. Second, many risk tolerance questionnaires will ultimately identify your maximum risk tolerance, not the risk level you are comfortable with so you can sleep at night with confidence. You should build your portfolio with a lower risk tolerance than what the questionnaire identified.

## Time Horizon

Not only is time horizon a key portfolio allocation input, it is also a cornerstone principle of asset allocation, and rightfully so, given the important role it plays. Time horizon greatly impacts expectations for asset class returns, asset class volatility, and correlations among asset classes.

The primary use of time horizon is to help you determine the portfolio balance between equities and fixed-income, namely bonds and cash. The general rule is the longer your time horizon the more equity assets and fewer fixed-income assets you should allocate to.

The most prevalent type of risk you need to address over the long term is purchasing power risk, or the loss of an asset's real value due to inflation. Equity investments provide the best hedge against this type of risk. In the short term, the most prevalent risk is price volatility. Fixed-income investments provide the best hedge against this type of risk.

## Income and Liquidity Needs and Preferences

Your needs for current income and liquidity will affect how you allocate your portfolio. This income addresses the degree to which you require cash to accomplish everyday activities and make special purchases. Consider, for example, a retired couple who uses their investment portfolio to fund their retirement. In this situation, the retired couple would have a much higher liquidity and income need than would a couple in their prime earning years when their income exceeds their expenses. As a result, the retired couple would need to build a portfolio that emphasizes income-oriented investments.

## Tax Status and Tax Considerations

This input variable is central to deciding what asset classes to invest in. One of the primary purposes is to aid in deciding what type of fixed-income securities to buy, namely taxable or tax-exempt. For taxable portfolios, investors with high federal tax rates will find it more appropriate to invest in tax-exempt investments rather than taxable investments. Tax-exempt portfolios should focus on taxable investments since the benefit of employing tax-exempt securities will be eliminated.

In addition to aiding in the decision to buy taxable or tax-exempt investments, this input will assist with the complex project of realizing, deferring, and avoiding taxes for the benefit of your portfolio. In consequence, *tax management* has become one of the hot new buzzwords in portfolio management. This is justifiably so since it can reduce portfolio performance by a substantial amount via capital gains taxes. In response, taxes and their impact on your portfolio should be one of the inputs employed when allocating your assets. As the number and complexity of your tax issues increase, so too does the need to involve either a certified public accountant (CPA) or an estate planning attorney.

The following are three of the tax categories you should familiarize yourself with and address in your portfolio.

- *Capital gains*: Capital gains taxes are taxes on the appreciation of an investment. Decisions to liquidate investments need to be evaluated with respect to their specific tax implications. However, investment decisions take utmost priority over tax considerations. For example, it is not prudent to hold an inappropriate investment just to defer the capital gains tax.
- *Growth versus income*: As with capital gains, deciding between growth-oriented and income-oriented investments should first be made at the investment level and then evaluated with respect to their tax implications. Simply allocating more to growth-oriented investments in order to avoid taxes on current income is not prudent if you have a short-term time horizon.
- *Tax-exempt investments*: Depending on your combined tax rate, it may be ideal to substitute lower-yielding tax-exempt government investments for higher-yielding taxable investments, for example, municipal bonds for corporate bonds. Why? The reason is because the net after-tax return might be higher with lower-yielding tax-exempt investments than with higher-yielding taxable investments since the latter is taxed. Adding more tax-exempt investments will decrease current income but might increase your portfolio's total after-tax return.

## Legal and Regulatory Considerations

Legal and regulatory considerations are much more prevalent with institutional investors than with individual investors. However, some of the legal and regulatory considerations you may encounter involve IRA contributions and withdrawals, employee stock option exercises, restricted stock, and insider trading. You may have to consider some of these input variables at some time in your investing career.

## Unique Preferences and Circumstances

This portfolio allocation input essentially incorporates anything that cannot be categorized in one of the other inputs, but still impacts how you should allocate your portfolio. Many of the items incorporated in this input are uniquely specific to the individual investor. These items can range in depth and breadth and may not be common to other investors. Examples of unique circumstances and preferences include the following items:

- Financially supporting a dependent parent or challenged adult child
- Excluding investments in defense, tobacco, or foreign companies
- Restricted from certain investments due to job or public service
- Filing for bankruptcy or having excessive debt

# Investment-Centric Inputs

## Correlations

Correlation is used to measure and convey how the prices of two investments move in relation to each other. Your task is to target asset classes that exhibit low, if not negative, correlations with other asset classes. Equities typically have correlations that are most different from the other asset classes. Therefore, allocating to equities, fixed-income, and alternative assets may be a wise decision.

## Expected Total Returns

Building an optimal portfolio requires knowledge and use of both current and expected future returns. Without this knowledge and ability to model in expected returns, you might design a portfolio where expected returns are not adequate to reach your performance aspiration. I use the term *total returns* instead of simply saying *returns* because I want to emphasize that returns comprise both price appreciation and income earned from interest and dividends.

## Risk Management Opportunities

It is important that investors have an understanding of how to manage and control risk with each investment. This is important because the greater the opportunities to manage risk, the greater the potential to maximize return for the level of risk. Without the management of risk, an investor may build a portfolio with too much risk warranted by his or her risk profile. By far, the primary opportunity is an asset class or investment that offers multiple investments with similar risk-and-return trade-off profiles. Investing in a basket or pool of similar investments minimizes investment-specific risk, or that risk from individual investments. Other opportunities for managing risk are the availability of derivatives and the ability to employ them.

## Inherent Volatility

As with investors, asset classes can be quite different. Even within the same asset class you will find differences, some quite significant. The most important market-centric input is inherent volatility. *Inherent volatility* is the degree to which the price of an investment changes due to specific characteristics that by definition are inherent in each investment. Greater inherent volatility translates into greater risk and may add more risk to your portfolio. Factors that impact volatility that each investment possesses include the following:

- Industry or sector
- Sensitivity to interest rates
- Sensitivity to changes in interest rates
- Float or shares outstanding
- Degree of uncertainty in expected returns

## Type of Returns

Are you looking for growth or income? How about deferred or immediate earnings? Each asset class can be classified as either providing current income, market value appreciation, or some combination of the two. In consequence, it is important to determine if certain investments match your needs or desire for current income. For instance, S&P 500 exchange-traded funds (ETFs) typically pay current income based on the dividends of the stocks in the S&P

500. Conversely, growth stocks typically pay little to no dividends as they prefer to reinvest their income. For investors desiring current income, it is important to know the differences among asset classes.

### Trading Flexibility

You will soon discover, if you have not already, that some investments are much easier to trade than others. Depending on their inherent nature, some will be more liquid than others and some will have more trading costs than others. In addition, some asset classes are more difficult to invest in due to their availability, such as micro caps, small caps, emerging markets investments, and commodities. There has been an explosion in exchange-traded funds over the last few years because they can solve the problem of inflexible trading.

### General Nature

Aside from liquidity, trading costs, and availability mentioned previously, asset classes also differ in regard to size, differentiation, definability, and completeness. Small differences between asset classes may be immaterial when determining your asset allocation. However, large and small differences may create a scenario where the asset class is considered fundamentally different from others. Allocating to fundamentally different asset classes is ideal.

## Common Portfolio Allocation Methods

Once your objectives and constraints are determined, your next task is to work toward allocating your assets suitable to your objectives. This task involves allocating assets to specific asset classes and asset subclasses that will enable you to build your optimal asset allocation.

Creating your own asset allocation is much like baking your own pie. You will first decide on the purpose of the pie—perhaps for Christmas, New Year's, or for a potluck. Once you have the purpose established, you will then narrow down what kind of pie you will make. Then you will need to identify what ingredients you will need and how best to bake your pie. Your choices of ingredients can vary widely from apple, pumpkin, lemon, or blueberry. Toppings also can be added for extra zing. When you are finished, you have a pie that fits the occasion.

Much the same process is used to determine your asset allocation and build your portfolio. The purpose for building your portfolio can vary widely, but most encompass some sort of retirement savings. Thereafter you will need to select the proper asset classes. There are many methods for accomplishing this task. Chapters 11, 12, and 13 will provide more information on model portfolios for different age groups.

The most common methods used by investors and investment professionals include equity overload, simple 110, cash flow matching, risk avoidance, allocation timing, and custom combination. All of these models have their advantages and disadvantages. None is absolutely perfect. A discussion of each method is provided below.

## Equity Overload

Notwithstanding risk, equity assets have outperformed all other primary asset classes over time. Within equities, small-cap stocks have performed better than blue chip stocks. This is the rationale that many investors and financial professionals use as support for a portfolio with nearly all equity, if not all equity. As long as an investor has a long-term time horizon, overloading to equities can be a way to earn solid portfolio performance over time. Beware, however! Since this method does not take risk into account, the volatility can be extraordinary and the risk of substantial loss uncommonly high. Not for the faint of heart.

## Simple 110

This is one of the most commonly recognized methods for determining asset allocations. However, I have slightly remodeled it for 110 rather than the traditional 100. Under this model, you allocate to equities based on the equation 110 minus your age. The remaining portion is allocated to fixed-income. For example, a 65-year-old investor would allocate 45 percent to equities (110 – 65) and the remaining 55 percent to fixed-income.

The underlying assumption of this model is that the investor will live well into retirement years and that his or her risk tolerance will decline with each passing year. The obvious drawback to this method is that it does not take into account many unique factors, such as risk tolerance, risk capacity, need to assume risk, and level of wealth.

## Cash Flow Matching

Cash flow match attempts to match your anticipated future financial obligations (your cash outflows) with your anticipated cash inflows, both noninvestment income and investment income. The first step in this model is to identify all anticipated future financial obligations. The second step is to identify all anticipated future financial inflows from noninvestment sources. Some sources of noninvestment income include wages, social security, and inheritance. Once these two steps have been accomplished, the third step will then be to determine the gap between the two. The fourth step is to evaluate your current portfolio against what will be needed from your portfolio in the future to fill the gaps in cash flows. This evaluation will determine what performance you will need to achieve, whether that means growth or preservation. For example, an investor determines that he will need to earn 10 percent per year in his portfolio for his retirement. Since corporate bonds have historically earned less than 10 percent annually whereas equities have historically earned greater than 10 percent annually, the investor will need to allocate some to equities and some to corporate bonds. Other combinations of high-yield bonds, small-cap stocks, international equities, and real estate investment trusts can be included as well.

The key is to match anticipated cash outflows with anticipated cash inflows and identify if your portfolio is large enough to fill the gap. If the gap between what you will need and what your noninvestment sources can provide is small, a small conservative portfolio may be appropriate. Although an investor may have the tolerance and capacity to assume risk, he or she may not have the need to assume additional risk, especially unnecessary risk that will provide no benefit.

Forecasting skill, life expectancy, and uncontrollable market factors are some of the drawbacks of employing this asset allocation method.

## Risk Avoidance

Regardless of risk capacity and return need, some investors simply do not want to take risk. They can't stomach it. As a result, allocating to conservative assets may be the most appropriate thing to do. Although investors in this situation may not be in the best position to accomplish their goals and objectives, they surely will sleep better at night. This gets at the root of behavioral finance and investing.

## Allocation Timing

Under this model, an investor or portfolio manager will change asset allocations in the hope of capturing short-term profits on asset classes showing the most strength. This is a timing strategy that numerous studies have shown to be fraught with errors, and the studies conclude that they rarely work. The allocation timing method involves allocating to asset classes when they are out of favor, such as equities during bearish stock markets, with the hope of selling at the peak of when they are in favor, such as during bullish stock markets. Information, care, and the skills needed for making such calls are absolutely critical for success.

### Custom Combination

Since many of the methods discussed above have one or more drawbacks, developing a custom combination may therefore prove quite beneficial. Many financial professionals have gone this route and designed their own unique method that uses the best from one or more of the methods. The vast majority employ some sort of cash flow matching combined with an allocation timing method. Doing so allows financial professionals to establish an asset allocation best suited for their investors while allowing them to promote their care and skill in portfolio management. Using a custom combination may be a smart move for you, depending on your situation. For example, at my company, we employ our own custom combination method called *Core & Opportunity*. Under this method, most of the portfolio is allocated according to the strategic asset allocation strategy where allocations are relatively fixed and stable over time. This describes the *Core* element in Core & Opportunity. A smaller segment of the portfolio is allocated to exchange-traded funds that are considered to offer the greatest probability of increasing in price over the upcoming 12 months. This describes the *Opportunity* element in Core & Opportunity. Many financial advisory firms offer their own unique method to ensure you do your due diligence before signing on.

The section below and Chapter 10 discuss some of the finer points to consider when determining your asset allocation.

## Ten-Step Plan for Allocating Assets

Although the process of allocating your assets may at first appear to be daunting, it is simpler than you might think. As you will notice, this 10-step plan is a custom combination method as described above. The primary process is to identify what financial goals and obligations you anticipate having in the future and the resulting cash outflows, what your cash inflows will be, and how best to design a portfolio that bridges the gap over time. The broad steps of asset allocation can be divided into 10 steps, each playing an important role in designing a winning portfolio. The 10-step plan for allocating your assets is discussed below.

### Step 1: Gather Relevant Financial Information

In order to identify your current and expected future financial position, prepare a plan and implement that plan to build a winning portfolio. First, you must gather all relevant financial information. This information includes brokerage statements, bank account statements, tax returns, trust or estate documents, and any other necessary documents.

## Step 2: Establish SMART Goals

Once you have gathered all relevant financial information, the next step is to establish your goals as they relate to your financial situation. Perhaps you want to retire at age 55, take a trip around the world at age 40, or put all of your children through an Ivy League college. These are very relevant goals that need to be taken into consideration when designing your portfolio and determining the most appropriate asset allocation to achieve your goals. The best goals to establish are smart goals. SMART is an acronym used as a mnemonic to help you remember the five characteristics of well-designed goals.

- *Specific*: Your goals should be unambiguous, clear, and well-defined.
- *Measurable*: Your goals should be quantifiable and calculable.
- *Accepted*: Your goals should be acknowledged and motivational.
- *Realistic*: Your goals should be achievable and attainable, not lofty.
- *Time-centric*: Your goals should be for a set period, nothing indefinite.

## Step 3: Identify Your Risk Profile and Financial Constraints

Your risk profile will play a significant role in determining what asset allocation is best for you. Risk profile encompasses three areas: your tolerance for risk, your capacity for risk, and your need to assume risk. Much the same as an army that moves only as fast as its slowest unit, the risk designed into your asset allocation will be based on the lowest amount of your tolerance, capacity, and need.

Once you have identified your risk profile, you then should give strong consideration to any material financial constraints that could help or hinder the building of your portfolio. Such financial constraints may be the need for significant liquidity to pay an unusual expense such as estate taxes, the desire to target tax-exempt investments given a high total tax bracket, or the need to invest in the short term for any number of reasons. Your asset allocation should accommodate any material financial constraint you may have.

## Step 4: Anticipate Future Cash Flows

Your job in this step is to identify all cash inflows and cash outflows that you reasonably expect to occur over the long term. Cash outflows are the result of funding financial obligations, such as college tuition or paying prescription drug costs, and goals that impact you financially, such as buying a vacation home, or joining the country club of your choice. Conversely, cash inflows are typically considered noninvestment income, such as wages and salaries, inheritance, business income, and social security. Identifying cash flows will give your investing a purpose.

## Step 5: Match Cash Flows and Identify Gaps

Once you understand what your anticipated future cash flows will be, you must next identify the gaps in cash outflows and cash inflows. Again we are talking about noninvestment cash inflows. Matching your outflows with inflows is certainly a good result, but most investors will not experience this. As a consequence, you will need to identify any gaps in cash flows over time.

## Step 6: Review Your Current Portfolio

Any gaps that you identified in Step 5 must be plugged with investment-related cash flows for your portfolio. If your portfolio is currently large enough to accommodate the cash flow gap, then your task of allocating assets is straightforward, and you would allocate your portfolio to relatively conservative asset classes, namely fixed-income. However, if your portfolio is not large enough at the current time to fund the cash flow gap, then your job will be to allocate assets that will generate target and reasonable returns to grow your portfolio over time.

## Step 7: Prepare a Plan and Design Your Portfolio

Once you have a solid understanding of your goals, financial constraints, gaps in cash flows, and current financial position, you will need to prepare a plan and design a portfolio that best achieves your goals. The first task is to identify your optimal asset allocation, or the primary asset classes to which you will allocate your portfolio: equities, fixed-income, cash, and alternative assets. The next task is to select asset subclasses, such as large-cap equities, small-cap value equities, international bonds, and high-yield bonds. The remaining task is simply to identify what type of investment you will use to build your portfolio. Your options include individual stocks, mutual funds, index funds, or perhaps even managed money. Remember, however, that reoptimizing your portfolio is more important than your initial asset allocation. Many people forget this key point.

## Step 8: Draft an Investment Policy Statement

An investment policy statement (IPS) is your plan in writing. Hence, there is no confusion as to what you are attempting to accomplish and how you are going to accomplish it. Your investment policy statement will detail many specific items about your current portfolio and situation and the portfolio you designed. An IPS will help keep your plan on track and help build and manage your portfolio over time.

## Step 9: Implement Your Investment Plan

Here you will put your plan into action. Under this step you will select a bro-kerage firm, if you do not already have one, and purchase your investments as dictated by your investment policy statement. Again, you might purchase individual stocks or mutual funds. Given their substantial diversification, liquidity, and low management costs, I highly encourage exchange-traded funds. They are the investment vehicle of choice at my firm.

## Step 10: Monitor and Reoptimize Your Portfolio

Since the assets in your portfolio will change over time due to price fluc-tuations, this step involves reoptimizing your portfolio to ensure it remains optimal and best positioned to achieve your financial goals and objectives. Reoptimization is comprised of four tasks. The Four Rs of Reoptimization include reevaluating, rebalancing, relocating, and reallocating. *Reevaluating* is the task of examining changes to your situation and financial position and modifying your portfolio accordingly. *Rebalancing* is the task of selling and buying investments with the goal of returning your current asset allocation to your optimal asset allocation. Rebalancing involves selling a portion of those asset classes that have become overweighted and buying a portion of those asset classes that have become underweighted. *Relocating* is the task of exchanging certain assets for other assets without changing the overall asset mix or risk-and-return trade-off profile. Relocating might involve exchanging a certain bond to obtain a higher or lower current rate of income or to obtain tax ben-efits. Finally, *reallocating* should be considered. This is the task of adjusting both where and in what proportion your contributions go to the asset classes in your portfolio. More specifically, you should contribute a greater amount to those asset classes that now have a lower allocation and contribute a lower amount to those asset classes that have gained in allocation.

---

In the next chapter, you will learn about the master asset allocation plan. It will be a blueprint for your winning portfolio.

# 10

# Master Asset Allocation Plan: Blueprint for Winning Portfolios

## Overview of Your Master Plan

Now that you have identified your portfolio allocation inputs, selected the most appropriate portfolio allocation method, and worked through the 10-step plan for allocating your assets, we now shift our attention to outlining the master asset allocation plan for bringing it all together and making it all happen. This is the point where action replaces reflection. This chapter will cover the implementation and management of your asset allocation.

Your optimal asset mix should be established to deliver a specific risk-and-return profile. As discussed in previous chapters, the appropriate risk-and-return profile is based on your objectives and constraints. For example, an investor with a moderate risk profile and long-term time horizon could have 60 percent in equity investments, 25 percent in fixed-income investments, 10 percent in cash and equivalents, and 5 percent in alternative assets. In contrast, an investor with a moderate risk profile but short-term time horizon could have 40 percent in equity investments, 35 percent in fixed-income investments, 25 percent in cash and equivalents with no alternative assets. Portfolios differ because of different objectives and constraints.

Once you have established your objectives and constraints, focus is then shifted to building and managing your winning portfolio. A properly designed portfolio is one that stands the best chances of achieving your goals within the context of your objectives and constraints. In other words, your goal is to implement and manage the portfolio that maximizes your total rate of return given the level of risk you can assume. To accomplish this goal, you will first need to address some considerations relating to implementing and managing your portfolio.

## Your Allocation Range Plan

Since it is not feasible to rebalance your portfolio every time an asset class weighting deviates from its optimal weighting, allocation ranges need to be established. Allocation ranges define the acceptable range that asset allocation percentages are allowed to change without rebalancing.

Allocation ranges are not necessarily the same for every investor. Rather, they can be narrow, moderate, or wide, depending on the desired degree of flexibility. For instance, an optimal asset mix with 60 percent in equity investments could have an allocation range of 50 to 70 percent for a low flexibility approach or 55 to 65 percent for a high flexibility approach. There is no firm rule for how much flexibility to incorporate. However, a good solution is to match the degree of flexibility to your risk profile. Thus, for more aggressive investors, more flexibility is desirable, thus establishing wider ranges. Conversely, for more conservative investors, less flexibility is desirable. As a result, the allocation ranges for a conservative investor will be much narrower and thus not allow the asset classes to sharply increase in price, thereby becoming overly risky for his or her situation.

## Your Liquidity Plan

There are times when investors with the same risk profile have different liquidity needs. As a result, you will need to address this by allocating a greater or lesser amount of each asset class to investments with higher interest and dividend yields. If two investors have identical risk profiles but different liquidity needs, then simply changing their optimal asset mixes to address this difference is not always prudent. Investments within each asset class or asset subclass should be changed first. For example, the optimal asset mix of an investor with a higher need for liquidity should not be modified to allow for a substantially lower allocation to equities and a substantially greater allocation to fixed-income investments. Rather, the equity and fixed-income investments should be selected to provide a higher dividend yield than the equity and fixed-income investments of the investor with a lower liquidity need. Remember, changing your optimal asset mix will change your risk-and-return trade-off profile.

There are four main categories of liquidity needs that you need to address: emergency cash, special needs, taxes, and savings and investments.

- *Emergency cash*: Having an emergency cash fund is by far the most important liquidity need you have. Conventional wisdom says this fund should amount to anywhere between three to six months of your average monthly expenses.
- *Special needs*: Special needs are essentially those purchases or expenditures that are planned sometime within the next three to eight years. Examples include a second home or college tuition.
- *Taxes*: There are two major taxes you will need to plan for: income taxes and estate taxes. Regardless of which tax, Uncle Sam wants his money quickly and we all must comply.
- *Savings and investments*: Savings and investments should not be mistaken for emergency cash. Each has its own purpose. Savings and investments allow you to take advantage of excess cash by forgoing current consumption and earning a return by putting it to work.

## *Your Management Style Plan*

There are two styles in which you can manage your portfolio's assets. The first is called *passive management* and the second is called *active management*. Passive management emphasizes index funds, both index mutual funds and exchange-traded index funds.

• • • • • • • • • • • • • • • • • • • • • • • • • • • • • • •

*Index Funds:* A mutual fund designed to match its return to a specific underlying index, such as the S&P 500 or Dow Jones Industrials Average.

• • • • • • • • • • • • • • • • • • • • • • • • • • • • • • •

*Exchange-Traded Funds (ETFs):* A mutual fund designed to match its return to that of a specific underlying index, such as the S&P 500 or Dow Jones Industrials Average. ETFs trade on a stock exchange rather than being issued by traditional mutual fund companies as are index funds.

• • • • • • • • • • • • • • • • • • • • • • • • • • • • • • •

The aim of passive management is to design a well-diversified portfolio quickly and easily without attempting to outperform the market via security selection. Over the last few years, there has been a proliferation in the number of index funds available to the individual investor. Investing in index funds is a quick and easy way to build a well-diversified portfolio at low cost. Most index investments have management fees under 0.40 percent. The same cannot be said for actively managed funds.

Active management, on the other hand, attempts to beat the market by employing security selection and market timing. As we know, security selection and market timing explain a portion of investment performance, but only marginally. By employing active management, you are betting that either you or your portfolio manager has the skills and talents to beat the market consistently. Lastly, since active management requires greater resources, you must pay to play. I highly encourage you to select passive management.

## Your Investment Style Plan

Investment style addresses how you should allocate and manage your equity assets between growth and value. Investment style is another method whereby you can enhance your risk-and-return profile.

The vast majority of equity securities can be classified as either growth stocks or value stocks. As with asset classes, the securities in each group tend to move together. Thus, when one growth stock is performing strongly, so too do other growth stocks, for the most part. This isn't always the case, but there is a solid positive correlation among the stocks in the group. The same goes for value stocks as well.

So why is this so important? Going back to the fundamentals of asset allocation, investments that are not perfectly, positively correlated provide the benefit of increased return and reduced risk. Since growth and value stocks are not perfectly, positively correlated, allocating to both asset classes is very desirable.

## Your Market Capitalization Plan

The investments within each market capitalization asset class (micro, small, middle, and large) tend to move together. At times, small-cap stocks will increase in price, whereas at other times, large-cap stocks will increase in price. To capture the correlation benefits of market capitalization, you should allocate a portion of your equity investments to multiple capitalization classes, preferably large-cap and small-cap stocks.

## Your International Plan

By including international assets to your investment portfolio, you add a new level of sophistication to your risk-and-return trade-off profile. At the same time, you are also able to enhance the expected return of your portfolio while decreasing risk. Why? The reason is because international assets have less than perfect correlations with domestic assets. As you know, less than perfectly positively correlated assets provide much desired benefits to the risk-and-return trade-off profile of your portfolio.

For those investors comfortable with international investments, purchasing shares of an index fund may be the most convenient and appropriate method for quick and easy exposure at a low cost. In Chapter 8 we discussed the benefits, costs, and risks of global asset allocation.

## Your Tax Plan

Since taxes on both capital gains and on interest and dividends can have such a drastic impact on the performance of your portfolio, it is necessary to define how you should plan for this contingency.

If your portfolio is tax-exempt, then tax management is more or less irrelevant. However, if your portfolio is not tax-exempt, then you need to place emphasis on tax management issues. Depending on your federal tax bracket, the focus might call for more tax-exempt fixed-income securities or more corporate fixed-income securities. In practice, investors with taxable portfolios and high tax brackets should emphasize tax-exempt fixed-income securities, such as municipal bonds and government agency bonds. Doing so will increase what is called the tax-equivalent yield.

*Tax-equivalent yield* can be defined as the yield you would receive given your tax rate if the income from your fixed-income security were taxable. Since in most cases you do not pay taxes on the interest from tax-exempt securities, your after-tax return is thus higher. Investors with lower tax brackets should consider taxable fixed-income securities since the tax bite will not be large enough to justify a lower-yielding tax-exempt security.

With capital gains, it is very important to consider the impact of taxes on the performance of your portfolio. Since asset allocation calls for investments in asset classes and different asset subclasses and not in select securities, you have the ability to offset capital gains by selling some securities with capital losses within the same asset class and then purchasing similar securities in the same asset class to replace them. The Internal Revenue Service (IRS) frowns upon selling securities strictly to realize a capital loss and buying back nearly identical securities. For example, the capital loss you realize from selling an

S&P 500 index may be disallowed by the IRS if you turn around and reinvest the proceeds of the sale within 30 days in the Dow Jones Industrials Average index. These two securities are nearly identical in the eyes of the IRS.

## Combining Opportunity Premiums

In Part Two we discussed asset class alternatives. Each chapter provided some specific opportunities to enhance your portfolio's performance potential. By combining specific risk-and-return premiums, you can take advantage of these opportunities to maximize your portfolio. For instance, allocating a portion of your portfolio to both large-cap stocks and corporate bonds will provide solid performance potential. However, combining large-cap stocks, corporate bonds, and small-cap stocks provides for even greater performance potential. Let's take this example even further. Combining large-cap stocks, corporate bonds, small-cap *value* stocks, and micro-cap stocks will greatly enhance your portfolio and lay the foundation for strong results over time. As you can see, taking advantage of multiple opportunity premiums is thus highly ideal and a no-brainer for an optimal portfolio. Solid performance potential is generated when proper allocations to asset classes with opportunity premiums are combined. Make every effort to accomplish this in your own portfolio.

## Portfolio Construction

There are four primary methods to construct your optimal portfolio. These four methods include *individual securities*, *separately managed accounts*, *mutual funds*, and *index funds*.

Deciding which construction method to use is vastly less important than deciding which asset classes to employ. Consider, for example, someone planning a vacation. The hard part is deciding where, when, and how. Once this is decided, actually going on the vacation is much easier. Depending on how you will address the aforementioned concepts, specifically management style, the decision of which construction method to employ could be more or less already made. A decision to employ passive management will automatically eliminate individual securities, separately managed accounts, and actively managed mutual funds from the equation. Each of the construction methods has its own advantages and disadvantages.

### Individual Securities

Individual stocks provide the best way to take advantage of security selection. Stocks can be screened and selected based on your judgment or the judgment of your portfolio manager. Unfortunately, this advantage is also a disadvantage if executed poorly. If the screens used or assumptions made regarding the expected returns of the securities are inaccurate, then the portfolio could perform poorly. If you decide to pursue this method, you may want to consider implementing a security selection system or method, such as the Dogs of the Dow system or programs offered by Value Line and Standard and Poor's.

## Separately Managed Accounts

Separately managed accounts, also commonly referred to as *wrap accounts*, have become very popular over the last several years. With separately managed accounts, an external portfolio manager handles all of the investment management responsibilities. Unlike mutual funds, separately managed accounts allow for more customized portfolios since the portfolio manager has firsthand knowledge of your objectives and constraints. Moreover, with separately managed accounts, the portfolio manager can tailor his or her management to your needs rather than the needs of thousands of investors, as mutual fund portfolio managers must do. The principal drawback to separately managed accounts is their higher fees. Higher fees are necessary to compensate for the specialized and customized management. Another drawback to separately managed accounts is their high initial minimums, typically around $100,000. Lastly, just because a portfolio is managed by a separate and external portfolio manager does not mean your portfolio will gain a performance advantage over other portfolios. Sometimes the performance of separately managed accounts will surpass the market and sometimes not. The performance depends on the skills of the portfolio manager. A little luck doesn't hurt either.

## Mutual Funds

Mutual funds provide many advantages, but also come with many disadvantages. Mutual funds provide professional management similar to separately managed accounts. The biggest advantages of mutual funds are their low minimums, significant liquidity, and means to easily and quickly build a well-diversified portfolio. Most mutual funds have small initial minimum investments, many around $1,000.

The biggest disadvantages of mutual funds are their high expenses, sometimes approaching 1.5 percent for equity mutual funds, and the excessive turnover of securities, which creates capital gain consequences. It is not uncommon for some aggressive mutual funds to turn over close to 90 percent of their holdings each year. Talk about little to no focus on tax management!

## *Index Funds*

Index funds have also become very popular over the last several years. They provide the means for investors to manage their portfolios passively. Most investors are gravitating to index funds as a way to reduce volatility in their investment portfolios. Index funds provide two important advantages. First and most obvious, they provide for a well-diversified portfolio. Index funds usually represent, or track, a market of some kind. For example, some index funds represent the market as a whole, such as the S&P 500, or represent specific industry groups, such as financials, pharmaceuticals, software, and semiconductors. With index funds, there is no need to worry about security selection as they represent all of the securities within that group.

The second advantage with index funds is their low annual management fees. Depending on the market that an index fund tracks and, to some degree, the market that the index fund sponsors, an index fund can have an annual management fee as low as 0.025 percent. That's four to six times lower than the management fees of most actively managed mutual funds.

The biggest disadvantage of index funds is their lack of ability to beat the market. Since they represent the market, by definition they cannot beat the market. This may be an issue with some investors, but successful investors realize that investing is not about taking significant risk day in and day out.

# Risk Avoidance Portfolio

Since not every investor has the desire or need to assume even conservative levels of risk, a risk avoidance approach may be suitable. Building a portfolio with risk avoidance is much different than with risk tolerance. Risk avoidance is a strategy where an investor purposely assumes less risk than he or she has capacity for. This scenario is much more common than you might think. The maximum level of risk you can assume is the highest value of either tolerance for risk, capacity for risk, or need for risk. Investors certainly do not want to assume risk if they don't need to. If you have accumulated enough assets to provide for the lifestyle and financial obligations you anticipate over your life, then there is no reason to assume your maximum level of risk. Doing so would be futile and foolish. As long as you have accumulated the amount of assets you will ever need or are on the path to accumulating the assets you will ever need, you do not need to invest at your peak risk tolerance.

Be mindful, however, that holding a portfolio that is overly conservative is not wise either. At risk is the principal of your portfolio to the negative

| Asset Class | Allocation |
|---|---|
| Equities | 20% |
| Fixed-Income | 65% |
| Alternative Assets (REITs) | 5% |
| Cash and Equivalent | 10% |

**Figure 10-1    Model Risk Avoidance Portfolio**

effects of taxes and inflation. Over time, both have the potential to substantially reduce overall portfolio value and reduce your future purchasing power. Keeping up with inflation should be the measuring yardstick. As such, allocating to intermediate-term and long-term bonds, with a small amount allocated to equities to defend against inflation and provide for higher returns, should provide a good balance.

For some investors, a risk avoidance portfolio is highly desirable to protect assets earned over their lifetime that otherwise could be harmed by the financial markets. A model risk avoidance portfolio is shown in Figure 10-1.

## Implementing Your Plan

This phase of the portfolio management process entails implementing the designed financial plan outlined in the investment policy statement (IPS) to build your desired optimal portfolio. The construction of your optimal portfolio is rather straightforward since the vast majority of your decisions have already been made during the design phase. At this stage, the process of constructing an optimal portfolio is much like the process of building a bookshelf. You simply need to read the instructions.

Of the four phases of portfolio management, the construction phase is the least time-consuming. The most difficult part of this phase is selecting investments that will comprise your portfolio. You must select investments within the context of the decisions you made during the design stage, such as whether to use active management or passive management and how much emphasis to place on international investments. Your job becomes even easier if you have decided to use index funds or mutual funds. Only when you have decided to use individual securities does your job of constructing your optimal portfolio become more time-consuming.

Aside from simply implementing the plan as designed in the previous phase, your significant task in the construction phase is to select a financial services firm to execute your transactions and hold your portfolio. You have many available choices from full-service firms to discount firms. Given the elimination of the Glass-Steagall Act of 1933, insurance companies and banks have now entered the investment business and can provide you with even more options.

# Monitoring Your Asset Allocation

## *Performance Monitoring*

Most portfolio managers evaluate the performance of a portfolio on a quarterly basis in order to appease the investor. However, evaluating portfolio performance is not as easy as it might initially appear. Why? First, there is the issue of evaluating a portfolio's short-term results when you have designed and implemented a long-term strategy. Only over longer periods of time can the benefits of asset allocation be measured. Any comparisons made using short-term periods are only measuring security selection and market timing, and nothing more. Second, it is difficult to compare a multi-asset-class portfolio to a benchmark. Which benchmark(s) do you select? Simply selecting the S&P 500 for a multi-asset-class portfolio will not suffice. The S&P 500 is comprised of equity securities only. Thus, a portfolio comprising fixed-income securities or alternative assets simply would not be appropriate. The solution is to segment each asset class and compare it against an appropriate benchmark, such as the S&P 500 for U.S. equity securities and the Europe, Australia, and the Far East markets (EAFE) for international equity securities.

One final thought about performance measurement and monitoring. It is very important to ensure that the performance data supplied by your portfolio manager, if you elect to use one, is created using geometric returns rather than arithmetic returns. Why? The reason is because the results can be totally misleading. For instance, let's say you invest $1,000,000 with a certain portfolio manager. During the following year, your portfolio suffers a huge loss and is worth $500,000. That's a negative 50 percent return. The following year your portfolio gains the $500,000 lost in the previous year, giving your portfolio a total market value of $1,000,000 at the end of the second year. Thus a return of 100 percent for year 2. Using arithmetic returns, your portfolio manager may claim to have earned you +25 percent (–50 percent + 100 percent divided by 2) during the two-year period. As you can see, your portfolio has not appreciated whatsoever, thus the +25 percent is not accurate. Using geometric returns, your portfolio manager would report a 0 percent return rather than a +25 percent return. This is something to keep in mind.

## Allocation Mix Monitoring

A portfolio's asset allocation mix must be compared periodically against your optimal asset mix and allocation ranges. Both parameters are established during the design phase. Deviations above or below the allocation range are grounds for rebalancing. Under strategic asset allocation, a portfolio manager may rebalance a portfolio if an asset class weighting were above or below range limits. However, tactical asset allocation is somewhat different. This strategy allows the portfolio manager to alter both the optimal asset mix and allocation ranges in the hope of capturing short-term profits. Consequently, monitoring and rebalancing of your portfolio has as much to do with the strategy selected as it does with your optimal asset mix and allocation ranges established.

# Rebalancing to Reoptimization

Over time, a portfolio's asset mix, including the resulting risk-and-return trade-off profile, will change due to price fluctuations, with some fluctuations being quite large. To address this issue, reoptimization may be needed. *Reoptimization* is comprised of four different, but somewhat similar tasks. These tasks, the Four Rs of Reoptimization, include *reevaluating, rebalancing, relocating*, and *reallocating*. Each is described below.

## Reevaluating

*Reevaluating* is the task of examining recent changes in your life in relation to your current portfolio. Many things may have changed in your life since you last designed and built your portfolio, and these could impact your SMART financial goals and risk profile. You may have changed jobs, married, divorced, had more children, or experienced a severe event in your life. As a result, you should take a long and hard look at your original financial plan and portfolio and modify if needed.

## Rebalancing

*Rebalancing* is the task of selling and buying investments in order to return a portfolio's current asset class mix to the previously established optimal asset mix. Rebalancing involves selling a portion of those asset classes that have become overweighted and buying a portion of those asset classes that have become underweighted. Rebalancing is key to maximizing a portfolio's risk-and-return trade-off profile over time.

## Relocating

*Relocating* is the task of exchanging certain assets for other assets without changing the overall asset mix or risk-and-return trade-off profile. Relocating might involve exchanging a certain bond to obtain a higher or lower current rate of income depending on a changed need for income. It also might involve switching to tax-exempt U.S. Treasury securities from taxable corporate bonds given a change in tax status resulting from greater taxable income.

## Reallocating

*Reallocating* is the task of adjusting which asset classes you make investment contributions to and in what proportion. In this context, reallocating does not change the mix of your assets, only how contributions will be made in the future.

## Benefits of Reoptimizing

The benefits of reoptimizing include the following:

- *Maximizes long-term performance*: Takes advantage of rotating asset class price leadership.
- *Minimizes short-term risk*: Rebalances out of more risky asset classes.
- *Returns the portfolio to the optimal asset mix*: Aligns the level of portfolio risk with your risk profile.
- Promotes the self-discipline to buy low and sell high: Delivers the right balance of risk and return.
- *Emphasizes anti–"follow the herd" mentality*: Following the crowd is the surest way to investment failure.
- *Promotes simple investment decisions*: Relocation and reallocation decisions are dictated by allocation need and SMART goals.
- *Makes selling decisions easy*: No more long and traumatic investment decisions.
- *Promotes uncomplicated portfolio monitoring*: Asset mix percentages are easy to calculate and evaluate.
- *Eliminates subjectivity and emotional selling decisions*: Your reoptimization moves are clearly defined and measured.

# Rebalancing Specifics

Rebalancing is the task of returning asset classes from current allocation mix to the optimal asset mix. Due to asset class price movements, some asset classes will need to be sold while others will need to be purchased. Rebalancing may be triggered if allocations move outside of the allocation range. This occurs when allocations move above established upper limits (ceilings) or below established lower limits (floors). Upper and lower limits are predicated on the allocation range flexibility established during the design phase. Lastly, although asset class allocations may be within the allocation range, rebalancing may occur at any time for various reasons if allocations deviate from your optimal asset mix.

## When to Rebalance

Sticking to your established asset mix during all times—good and bad—is more important than the initial task of establishing your optimal asset mix. Rebalancing may be triggered when asset class weightings move beyond previously established allocation ranges.

Some investment experts advocate rebalancing once per year rather than when asset weightings deviate from their respective allocation ranges. This approach fails to address asset weightings that may have deviated significantly from their optimal asset mix during the year. If someone is going to let his or her asset weighting deviate, then there is no reason to place any significant emphasis on determining the optimal asset mix since we know that market forces will change weightings and could do so drastically.

Lastly, you need to consider the possibility that your allocation range flexibility may be too narrow or too wide. This could determine what degree your asset allocation mix is allowed to deviate from your optimal asset mix before you rebalance.

## Changes to the Allocation Ranges

There are two principal reasons why you may need to modify your allocation ranges. These modifications include changes to your objectives and constraints and changes to asset class risk-and-return profiles. Changes impacting your objectives and constraints may come from specific financial goals, wealth, risk tolerance, time horizon, liquidity needs, tax considerations, legal and regulatory considerations, and unique circumstances and preferences. In addition, changes affecting asset class risk-and-return profiles may come from changes to asset class return potentials, changes in asset class risk potentials, macro-economic changes, and overall changes to the market portfolio.

## How Often Should Rebalancing Occur?

The frequency and degree of rebalancing is dependent on the occurrence and degree to which your asset class weightings deviate from your optimal asset mix. The wider you set your upper and lower allocation ranges, the less frequently you will have to rebalance. Conversely, the narrower the upper and lower allocation ranges, the more frequently you will have to rebalance. On the other hand, although you will have to rebalance less frequently with wider allocation ranges, the amount of rebalancing will be greater.

## Costs of Rebalancing

There are two chief costs you need to consider before rebalancing. The first is trading costs—bid-ask spread and commissions that are charged. Mutual fund loads are considered a transaction cost as well. The second is taxes on potential capital gains from the sale of securities. Depending on the cost basis, capital gains have the potential to dwarf transaction costs and all other costs associated with executing a sell transaction.

One note of caution: The costs of rebalancing should prompt you to take a short pause, not necessarily stop the process of rebalancing altogether. As mentioned earlier, decisions to sell a security or securities need to be evaluated with respect to their tax implications. However, investment decisions take utmost priority over tax considerations. It is not prudent to cease rebalancing simply to defer capital gains taxes.

# Smith Foundation Example

## Monitoring Observations

- Equity assets are over their upper limit by 5 percent; rebalancing may be needed.
- Fixed-income assets are under their lower limit by 5 percent; rebalancing may be needed.
- Cash and equivalents assets are within their allocation range; no rebalancing is needed.
- No allocation to alternatives.

## Rebalancing Actions

- Sell equity assets in the amount of 15 percent of the portfolio, which equates to about 27.3 percent of equity assets.
- Reallocate the proceeds of the sale to purchase fixed-income.

| Asset Class | Current Asset Allocation | Target Lower Limit | Optimal Asset Allocation | Target Upper Limit |
|---|---|---|---|---|
| Equities | 55% | 30% | 40% | 50% |
| Fixed-Income | 25% | 30% | 40% | 50% |
| Cash & Equivalents | 20% | 15% | 20% | 25% |
| Alternative Assets | --- | --- | 0% | --- |

**Figure 10-2    Rebalancing Example 1—Smith Foundation**

## Detailed Description

The Smith Foundation has an optimal asset mix of 40 percent equities, 40 percent fixed-income, and 20 percent cash and equivalents. For allocation ranges, the portfolio has 30 to 50 percent equities, 30 to 50 percent fixed-income, and 15 to 25 percent cash and equivalents. The portfolio employs strategic asset allocation. See Figure 10-2 for this rebalancing example.

Due to a semistrong equity market and semiweak fixed-income market, one year later the asset mix is comprised of 55 percent equities, 25 percent fixed-income, and 20 percent cash and equivalents. After evaluating the equity and fixed-income deviations, the portfolio manager decides to move forward with rebalancing. As a result, the portfolio manager sells approximately 27.3 percent of equities (which represents 15 percent of the portfolio's total market value) to return the equity weighting to the optimal asset mix. In addition the portfolio manager reallocates the proceeds of the equity sale to fixed-income, thus returning it to the optimal asset mix as well.

## Jones Foundation Example Monitoring Observations

* Equity assets are within their allocation range; no rebalancing is needed.
* Fixed-income assets are under their lower limit by 5 percent; rebalancing may be needed.

- Cash and equivalents assets are within their allocation range; no rebalancing is needed.
- Alternative assets are within their allocation range; no rebalancing is needed.

## Rebalancing Actions

- Buy 50 percent more fixed-income assets, which represents 10 percent of the total portfolio market value.
- Sell a portion of equities and alternative assets to fund the purchase of fixed-income securities.

## Detailed Description

The Jones Foundation has an optimal asset mix of 55 percent equities, 30 percent fixed-income, 10 percent cash and equivalents, and 5 percent alternative assets. For allocation ranges, the portfolio has 45 to 65 percent equities, 25 to 35 percent fixed-income, 7 to 13 percent cash and equivalents, and 3 to 7 percent alternative assets. The portfolio employs strategic asset allocation. See Figure 10-3 for this rebalancing example.

Due to strength in equities and alternatives and weakness in fixed-income, one year later the portfolio's asset mix is comprised of 63 percent equities, 20 percent fixed income, 10 percent cash and equivalents, and 7 percent

| Asset Class | Current Asset Allocation | Target Lower Limit | Optimal Asset Allocation | Target Upper Limit |
|---|---|---|---|---|
| Equities | 63% | 45% | 55% | 65% |
| Fixed-Income | 20% | 25% | 30% | 35% |
| Cash & Equivalents | 10% | 7% | 10% | 13% |
| Alternative Assets | 7% | 3% | 5% | 7% |

Figure 10-3    Rebalancing Example 2—Jones Foundation

alternatives. After evaluating the fixed-income deviation, the portfolio manager decides to move forward with rebalancing. As a result, the portfolio manager buys 50 percent more fixed-income (which represents 10 percent of the total portfolio market value) to return the fixed-income weighting to the optimal asset mix. In addition, the portfolio manager funds the fixed-income purchase by selling both equities and alternative assets. Cash and equivalents assets are not touched in this scenario.

# Investment Policy Statement

Much like a blueprint for building a house, an investment policy statement (IPS) serves as a blueprint for building a winning portfolio. The IPS is crucial to the long-term achievement of your specific financial goals. First and foremost, an investment policy statement helps you to learn more about what your needs and priorities are, how to best address them, and the risks involved with investing. Secondly, this policy allows you and your portfolio manager (if you elect to employ one) to gain a better understanding of your objectives and constraints and how to best manage your portfolio to accomplish your specific financial goals. Without an investment policy statement, a portfolio manager may make inappropriate investment decisions such as incorporating high-risk asset classes in an otherwise conservative to moderate risk portfolio or incorporating more fixed-income asset classes in a growth-oriented portfolio. This could result in a portfolio that underachieves its intended purpose or incorporates greater risk than appropriate.

An investment policy statement alone will not guarantee success in protecting and growing your winning portfolio. Rather, it will shelter your portfolio from ad hoc revisions, made either by you or your portfolio manager, from a sound long-term asset allocation policy.

## Outline of an Investment Policy Statement

A properly drafted investment policy statement outlines the asset classes selected for investment and their respective weightings within your portfolio. In addition, many policies also make mention of security selection and timing strategies. A properly drafted investment policy statement clearly articulates your objectives and constraints as well as how to address and incorporate them within the portfolio management process.

Your IPS should make every effort to incorporate the following:

- Your current portfolio
- Your objectives and constraints

- Recommended (or desired) portfolio
- Portfolio construction process
- Portfolio monitoring process
- Portfolio rebalancing process
- Annual review process
- Agreement between you and your portfolio manager

## Benefits of an Investment Policy Statement

Articulating your specific financial goals, objectives, and constraints provides a benchmark, or objective standard, with which to evaluate your portfolio manager. For example, clearly specifying in the investment policy statement which asset classes or asset subclasses to incorporate will allow for the selection of an appropriate benchmark, such as the S&P 500, Wilshire 5000, or Goldman Sachs Corporate Bond Fund. A portfolio comprising low-risk asset classes should be compared against low-risk benchmarks, while portfolios with high-risk asset classes should be compared against high-risk benchmarks. Once the benchmarks are selected, you will be able to compare the performance of your portfolio manager against the indices, or alternatively what you could earn through passive, rather than active, portfolio management. The greater the positive deviation between the return of your portfolio and the return of the appropriate benchmark, the more value your portfolio manager has added. Conversely, the greater the negative deviation, the more value the portfolio manager has destroyed. In that scenario we all know what usually results; it's time for a new portfolio manager.

An investment policy statement also helps to curb unethical behavior on the part of your portfolio manager. Given that your objectives and constraints are clearly spelled out in written form for all interested parties, miscommunications or actions such as playing the market or taking unnecessary chances, are not only easier to discover but also much less likely to occur.

Another significant benefit of using an investment policy statement is when there is a change in portfolio managers. Due to many reasons, occurring both within the investment firm and with the portfolio manager, most portfolio managers will manage your portfolio for only a short period of time. Since your time horizon may extend out 20 or more years, one can easily visualize the large number of portfolio managers you may have. As a result, an investment policy statement will ensure a smooth transition from portfolio manager to portfolio manager. The new portfolio manager will be able to jump right in where the previous portfolio manager left off, thus reducing any potential delays in monitoring and rebalancing your portfolio and promoting consistency of management.

The investment policy statement may take many forms, from simple asset class targets to highly complex and often specific criteria. Some policy statements may even state which investments a portfolio manager is prohibited from incorporating, such as real estate, commodities, derivatives, or foreign bonds. The written IPS will assist you to maintain a long-term approach when short-term market volatility may bring about sleepless nights and misgivings about the plan. In the past, only institutional investors had used investment policy statements. However, due to its many benefits, it is now common for individuals to use an IPS as well.

## Summary of IPS Benefits

- Assists you to more fully understand what your specific financial goals are and how best to prioritize them
- Assists the portfolio manager to understand what your objectives and constraints are and how to best manage your portfolio
- Outlines your optimal asset mix, asset allocation strategy, and construction method (sometimes including security selection and timing)
- Establishes what management style, investment style, and market capitalization style your portfolio manager must employ
- Provides a benchmark or benchmarks with which to evaluate the performance of your portfolio manager
- Guards the portfolio against any ad hoc decisions that will impede your long-term strategy
- Greatly decreases miscommunications and misunderstandings and allows for such occurrences to be quickly and easily resolved

## Updating Your Investment Policy Statement

An investment policy statement should be reviewed and, if appropriate, modified at least annually. A comprehensive review of your return aspirations, risk tolerance, liquidity needs, time horizon, legal considerations, and unique circumstances and preferences should be made and any changes incorporated into the existing policy. It is your responsibility to communicate to your portfolio manager any and all changes to your financial position as soon as possible. Doing so will help your portfolio manager work toward achieving your specific financial goals and objectives.

In the next chapter, you will learn about the early accumulators' life-cycle group and related model portfolios for long-term appreciation.

# 11

# Early Accumulators: Model Portfolios for Long-Term Appreciation

## Profile

Early accumulators are people typically in their early careers with long-term time horizons. Their net worth, and sometimes their income, is small relative to their debt. Most people in this group typically are in their educational years, be it high school or college, and may either rent or own their first or second homes. Many people in this group will have student loans, credit card debt, and be burdened by other debt payments. Although difficult to do, starting an investment plan in this phase of life is of primary importance. Some people will already have married and started raising a family. The goals for people in this life-cycle group are to begin paying down debt, start saving for retirement, and buy a home—an asset that will appreciate over time. A home is one of the best appreciable investments a person can make.

Other notes of primary importance are that people in this group have lower living expenses, although their economies of scale are much smaller. Paying for a mortgage or monthly rent is obviously much easier with two or more people than it is with just one. Another key factor revolves around having a family. Children will add a new complexity to early accumulators' financial situations whereby their expenses will go up and their need to save more will increase dramatically. Having a dual income will help to greatly offset any increase in expenses.

## Common Goals

Many people in this life-cycle group share similar goals and needs. Accordingly, many people in this group will establish very similar asset allocations and manage them in such a way as to match future financial funding obligations with investment returns. Some of the most common goals for people in this life-cycle group are the following:

- Establish a career
- Upgrade their vehicle
- Start or expand their family
- Begin saving for retirement
- Buy or upgrade a home
- Pay down student loans
- Increase liquidity and establish an emergency fund
- Begin saving for children's education

## Common Risks

Some of the more common risks associated with people in this life-cycle group are included below. As you will see, all of them affect personal finances to various degrees. Even people with similar goals and needs can have completely different experiences funding their retirement or traditional investment accounts, depending on their cash inflow and outflow. Early accumulators should avoid the following risks:

- Living a lifestyle that they cannot afford
- Incurring significant debt
- Failing to save for retirement
- Not establishing a financial plan
- Not being long-term career minded
- Spending money on frivolous items
- Failing to take advantage of employer retirement matching funds

# Common Objectives

## Portfolio Return Aspiration

With a long-term time horizon, people in the accumulation life-cycle phase should seek total returns by focusing their portfolios on capital gain, growth-oriented assets. At the same time, people in this phase need to be cognizant of current income to help with immediate spending goals.

## Risk Profile

Due to their long-term time horizon, people in this phase have the ability to tolerate a high level of risk. That being said, many people will not have the willingness or need to tolerate risk. It is very important that you identify your true risk profile to better enable you to develop a sound financial plan.

# Common Constraints

## Time Horizon

The time horizon for people in the early accumulators life-cycle phase is very long, sometimes as long as 70+ years. As a result, they can assume additional risk because they will have ample time to turn things around. Remember, the longer you hold an asset, especially equity assets, the greater the probability of a positive return over time. Lastly, time horizon is the key factor in determining your balance between equity and fixed-income assets. The longer your time horizon, the more emphasis you should place on equity assets. The shorter your time horizon, the more emphasis you should place on fixed-income assets. An intermediate time horizon will dictate a more balanced portfolio of equities and fixed-income assets.

## Income and Liquidity Needs

Early accumulators have a moderate to high need for liquidity given their immediate spending needs. Since many people in this life-cycle phase have a high need to make many purchases for their home, work, school, or career, spending will be typically high. The main objective is to minimize spending as much as possible to ensure an adequate amount of liquidity. It is critical to have an emergency fund.

## Tax Considerations

Estate, trust, and other tax considerations are low for early accumulators. The most important taxes to consider are capital gains and income. Given their long-term time horizon, and from a tax perspective, growth-oriented assets are preferable over income-oriented assets. However, the need for income-oriented assets must be balanced with growth-oriented assets to cover current spending needs.

## Legal and Regulatory Considerations

Most early accumulators will have very few legal and regulatory issues to contend with. The most common issues will be related to contributions and withdrawals from retirement accounts, namely IRAs and 401(k)s. Wills and related legal documents should be completed at this time.

## Unique Circumstances and Preferences

For early accumulators, unique circumstances and preferences could include single-parent families, financially supporting an adult parent, incurring large expenses from higher education, alimony payments, business start-up expenses, or paying child support.

# Optimal Asset Allocations

The optimal mix of assets for people in this life-cycle group will emphasize equity assets given their traditionally long-term time horizons. The allocation to equities can be additionally divided into U.S. equities and international equities. As always, you should emphasize total U.S. stock market index funds as well as international index funds for significant diversification and for a low-cost alternative. A smaller allocation should be made to fixed-income whereas alternative assets should be considered as well. Index funds can be used for both. Personally, I prefer exchange-traded funds over index mutual funds, but the choice is up to you. Finally, a cash reserve for emergency situations is ideal and highly encouraged.

# Model Portfolios

## Broad Asset Allocation Models

Figure 11-1 illustrates broad asset allocation models for three risk profiles: conservative, moderate, and aggressive. As you can see, conservative investors

| Asset Class | Conservative Investors | Moderate Investors | Aggressive Investors |
|---|---|---|---|
| Equities | 50% | 65% | 80% |
| Fixed-Income | 40% | 25% | 10% |
| Cash & Equivalents | 5% | 5% | 5% |
| Alternative Assets | 5% | 5% | 5% |

**Figure 11-1     Broad Asset Allocation Model Portfolios**

should allocate approximately 50 percent to equity investments, 40 percent to fixed-income investments, 5 percent to cash and equivalents investments, and 5 percent to alternative investments. Aggressive early accumulators, on the other hand, will allocate a greater amount to equity investments at the expense of lower return and lower risk potential fixed-income investments.

## Specific Asset Class Models

Figure 11-2 illustrates both the broad asset allocation classes and a more refined look at the asset subclasses. In addition, specific exchange-traded funds that I employ at my company are included for your reference. The allocation ranges presented are per the broad asset allocation models discussed above.

It is very important that you consider these model portfolios within the context of your own personal circumstances and objectives. Working with a professional financial advisor may provide additional guidance and value. Also, use these model portfolios as benchmarks and for comparisons to your present asset allocation.

# A Review

It is rather cut and dried with people in the accumulation life-cycle phase. Their portfolios should emphasize equity investments given their tradition-ally long-term time horizons. The allocation to equity investments will vary

| Asset Class | Allocation and Index Fund |
|---|---|
| **EQUITIES:** | **50 - 80%** |
| Total U.S. Stock Market | iShares Total U.S. Stock Market-IYY |
| Small Cap Value | iShares S&P SmallCap 600 Value-IJS |
| Micro-Cap | iShares Russell MicroCap-IWC |
| International | iShares MSCI EAFE-EFA |
| **FIXED-INCOME:** | **10-40%** |
| Total U.S. Bond Market | iShares Lehman Aggregate Bond Fund-AGG |
| High-Yield Bonds | Vanguard High-Yield Corporate-VWEHX |
| International Bonds | DFA Five-Year Global Fixed-Income-DFGBX |
| **CASH & EQUIVALENTS:** | **5%** |
| Money Markets | Treasury bills, savings or certificates of deposit |
| **ALTERNATIVES:** | **5%** |
| Real Estate | Cohen & Steers Realty Majors-ICF |

**Figure 11-2    Specific Asset Class Model Portfolios**

slightly depending on the risk tolerance of these investors. Aggressive investors will allocate a greater portion of their portfolios to equities whereas conservative investors will allocate less with a greater allocation to fixed-income.
Regardless of your risk profile, allocating to alternative assets, namely real
estate, and having a cash allocation is simply wise investing.

Your asset allocation will not remain static. It will change over time as
your financial situation and risk profile change. For example, earning a pro-
motion with a higher salary will increase your personal finances and should
motivate you to contribute a greater amount to your retirement savings. Your
portfolio allocation may need to be modified, or reoptimized, as a result.

Finally, early accumulators should place importance on creating a financial plan, one that will guide them and their portfolio over the long term in
order to achieve financial success. Drafting an investment policy statement
as early as possible is encouraged.

In the next chapter, you will learn about growth and preservation model
portfolios for the mid-life consolidators life-cycle group.

# 12

# Mid-Life Consolidators: Model Portfolios for Growth and Preservation

## Profile

People in this life-cycle group tend to be in their middle to late working years when their time horizon is still relatively long and their need for increased contributions to fund retirement savings and educational savings is high. As people progress through this phase, their income begins to exceed their expenses and therefore their capacity to make retirement and educational funding contributions goes up. Many people in this group have already achieved their highest level of education (although not always the case), and most are already at their peak earning years. This is truly the optimal time in one's life to make retirement and educational savings contributions. If not now, when?

A great many people in this group begin to wonder how much money it will take to sustain their desired level of spending and lifestyle into retirement. A good solution is to identify how much money you believe you will need each year during retirement based on what you are presently spending. Some people may want to adjust that figure up or down, depending on whether they believe their lifestyle will require more money or less. For example, will you be golfing more or less or will you be dining out more or less in retirement? After this step, identify all sources of noninvestment income per year. Any gaps between what you believe you will need per year and what noninvestment sources will provide is the amount per year you will need to plug with investment savings. A qualified financial planner can help you with this.

Mid-life consolidators will also want to focus on many noninvestment-related tasks to protect their future financial security. These tasks include, but are not limited to, drafting estate planning documents; verifying that you have adequate life, disability, and long-term care insurance; and gifting assets to reduce any potential estate tax bill.

## Common Goals

As with the early accumulators life-cycle group, mid-life consolidators also share similar goals, needs, and risks. Some of the most common include the following:

- Peaking in their career
- Putting their children through college
- Increasing contributions to retirement savings
- Upgrading to a new home
- Buying a vacation home
- Taking more vacations
- Opening a business
- Volunteering more time to charities
- Eliminating unsecured debt
- Allocating more time to leisure activities
- Deciding when and how best to retire

## Common Risks

Many of the common risks associated with people in this life-cycle group have to do with lack of planning, and they all impact personal finances to various degrees. It is very important to avoid these financial risks. The common risks confronting this group include the following:

- Failing to increase contributions for retirement savings
- Spending more money than what is earned
- Failing to plan accordingly for children's educational costs
- Not drafting estate planning documents
- Failing to obtain adequate insurance coverage
- Not giving more thought to desired retirement lifestyle and expenses

# Common Objectives

## Portfolio Return Aspiration

With a long-term time horizon, mid-life consolidators should seek total returns by focusing their portfolios on capital gains and growth-oriented assets. In addition, more emphasis should be placed on reallocating assets to less risky investments as they progress through this life-cycle phase. Although a small rebalancing out of equities to fixed-income should be made, it is important to keep a balanced approach between the two. For most mid-life consolidators, having around 50 percent in equities, 35 percent in fixed-income, 10 percent in alternatives, and 5 percent in cash and equivalents is ideal.

## Risk Tolerance

Due to their long-term time horizon, people in this phase have the capacity to tolerate an above average level of risk. Remember, however, that an investor's risk capacity and tolerance for risk need to be addressed within the context of the need to assume risk. Just because investors have the willingness and capacity to take more risk does not mean that they should. You may not need to assume additional risk to achieve your financial goals and objectives.

# Common Constraints

## Time Horizon

The time horizon for people in the mid-life consolidation life-cycle phase is long, anywhere from 20 to 40 or more years. In consequence, equities should be the predominant asset class in this group's portfolios. As people move through this phase, a slight relocation out of equities to fixed-income is usually a smart move. As mentioned previously, time horizon is by far the single most significant determinant for the allocation balance between equity and fixed-income assets.

## Income and Liquidity Needs

People in this phase have a low need for liquidity since their incomes tend to exceed their expenses. Even so, prudent investors should increase their contributions to not only retirement and educational savings but also expand their emergency fund. A good rule of thumb is to have an emergency fund that can fund between three and six months of expenses.

## Tax Considerations

Most tax considerations remain low for people in this group, but some new considerations begin to appear, such as trust taxes. As with the early accumulators, growth-oriented assets, namely equities, are preferable over fixed-income assets as a means of avoiding immediate tax consequences. An asset allocation buy and hold strategy will help to minimize tax implications by deferring otherwise immediate tax consequence to a future date when the assets are ultimately sold. Dividends and interest from bonds or blue-chip companies may be received and should be considered when designing and reoptimizing the optimal asset allocation of the mid-life consolidators.

## Legal and Regulatory Considerations

As people begin to approach retirement, their legal and regulatory issues occur more frequently. People in this phase will need to update their wills, ensure their insurance named beneficiaries are appropriate, and use adequate estate planning. One important note for people in this group is that penalty-free distributions from retirement plans cannot be made until age 59½.

## Unique Circumstances and Preferences

There are always a few unique circumstances and preferences that mid-life accumulators might face. For example, some of these might be forced early retirement, a changed family situation such as divorce, an additional financial obligation such as supporting an adult parent or disabled child, or bankruptcy from a failed business or unwise personal financial decisions.

# Optimal Asset Allocations

The optimal mix of assets for people in this life-cycle group, given their generally long-term time horizons, will emphasize equity assets. To enhance the risk-and-return trade-off profile of the portfolio, allocating to multiple asset classes is ideal. Specifically, allocating to small-cap value stocks and microcap stocks will provide both size and style premium benefits. In addition, allocating to both international developed equities and international emerging markets equities will maximize the portfolio's risk-adjusted return. Finally, the remaining equity allocation should be invested in a total U.S. stock market index fund. Index funds should be emphasized to provide both significant diversification and low cost. This low cost encompasses both low management fees and low tax implications.

An allocation to fixed-income investments is prudent as this will decrease volatility risk and enhance the risk-adjusted return. Alternative assets should be added with real estate investment trusts being the optimal pick. As with early accumulators, mid-life consolidators should also allocate about 5 to 10 percent to cash and equivalent investments.

# Model Portfolios

## Broad Asset Allocation Models

Figure 12-1 illustrates three broad asset allocation models for mid-life consolidators based on three risk profiles: conservative, moderate, and aggressive. As you will see, conservative investors should allocate approximately 30 percent to equity investments, 50 percent to fixed-income investments, 10 percent to cash and equivalents investments, and 5 percent to alternative investments. Aggressive early accumulators, on the other hand, will allocate about 60 percent of their portfolio to equities with only 25 percent going to fixed-income and the remaining 15 percent to alternative and cash investments.

## Specific Asset Class Models

Figure 12-2 provides both the broad asset allocation classes and a more refined look at the asset subclasses. Specific exchange-traded funds that I employ at my company are included for your reference to give you an idea of what to consider for your portfolio.

As always, it is vitally important to compare these and any model portfolio against your own personal financial situation, circumstances, and objectives. Employing a professional financial advisor may be a wise

| Asset Class | Conservative Investors | Moderate Investors | Aggressive Investors |
|---|---|---|---|
| Equities | 30% | 45% | 60% |
| Fixed-Income | 55% | 40% | 25% |
| Cash & Equivalents | 10% | 5% | 5% |
| Alternative Assets | 5% | 10% | 10% |

**Figure 12-1    Broad Asset Allocation Model Portfolios**

| Asset Class | Allocation and Index Fund |
|---|---|
| **EQUITIES:** | **30 - 60%** |
| Total U.S. Stock Market | iShares Total U.S. Stock Market - IYY |
| Small Cap Value | iShares S&P SmallCap 600 Value - IJS |
| Micro-Cap | iShares Russell MicroCap - IWC |
| International | iShares MSCI EAFE - EFA |
| **FIXED-INCOME:** | **25 - 55%** |
| Total U.S. Bond Market | iShares Lehman Aggregate Bond Fund - AGG |
| High-Yield Bonds | Vanguard High-Yield Corporate - VWEHX |
| International Bonds | DFA Five-Year Global Fixed-Income - DFGBX |
| **CASH & EQUIVALENTS:** | **5 - 10%** |
| Money Markets | Treasury bills, savings or certificates of deposit |
| **ALTERNATIVES:** | **5 - 10%** |
| Real Estate | Cohen & Steers Realty Majors - ICF |

**Figure 12-2    Specific Asset Class Model Portfolios**

move as he or she can help with keeping things objective and offer expertise beyond what most investors have. Chapter 16 gives you information on how to evaluate and select an appropriate financial advisor. The model portfolios in Figure 12-2 should be considered benchmarks for comparisons to your present asset allocation. Remember to modify your portfolio according to your unique personal financial situation, not based on what someone else has done.

# A Review

Given the traditionally long-term time horizons for people in the mid-life consolidators life-cycle group, equity assets should be the foundation regardless of risk profile. Depending on the risk profile, people in this group will want to allocate a somewhat larger amount of investments to fixed-income assets. Conservative mid-life consolidators should allocate the greatest amount to fixed-income securities to minimize volatility risk. As people age, a rebalancing from fixed-income to equity investments should be considered to align portfolio risk with investor risk capacity and/or risk need.

Reoptimizing your portfolio will be key to ensuring you have the optimal portfolio to achieve your goals and objectives. Reoptimizing your portfolio includes reevaluating, rebalancing, reallocating, and relocating. Over time your portfolio asset mix will change. A static portfolio is a sure sign of lack of portfolio reoptimizing activities.

Finally, mid-life consolidators need to address estate planning and ensure their retirement plan is appropriate. A qualified financial advisor or attorney can help with both tasks. Revising or drafting an investment policy statement is prudent for long-term success.

In the next chapter, you will learn about income and stability model portfolios for the Retired Spenders and Gifters life-cycle group.

# 13

# Retired Spenders and Gifters: Model Portfolios for Income and Stability

## Profile

This chapter discusses two very similar but somewhat unique life-cycle groups: retired spenders and retired gifters. The sole difference between these two groups is how to manage their portfolios given a desire to pass on assets upon death. At some point in time, many retirees will discover that they have more assets than they will ever need. Therefore, they will decide to gift some or all of their assets to heirs and/or charities either directly or via a charitable foundation. Since a retiree's portfolio must be managed differently depending on whether it will gift to an heir or to a charity or to both, a balance must be achieved to accommodate all scenarios.

People in this life-cycle group are in one of the three stages of retirement— early, mid, or late—with time horizons ranging anywhere from seven to twenty years or more. As a result, time horizons can vary from short term to long term. In addition, although a portfolio may be managed with the short term in mind, a change to a long-term approach can occur when the gifting of assets is desired. For example, if an investor had a $10 million portfolio and a desire to gift half of that amount to her alma mater in five years, then having that portfolio invested in only fixed-income might be a disservice to the beneficiary. Over that five-year period, the portion intended as a gift may grow more if at least some of it were invested in equity assets. Since universities have long-term time horizons themselves, so managing those assets targeted as gifts is prudent. Plus, a larger gift is a larger tax deduction for the gifter, if needed.

For many retirees, their expenses will exceed their noninvestment income in retirement, which obviously creates a scenario where retirement expenses will need to be supplemented by investment and retirement income. Having a portfolio asset allocation to accommodate this is thus highly warranted.

## Common Goals

Aside from a desire to transfer assets at death, retired spenders and gifters share similar goals, needs, and risks. Some of the most common goals include the following:

- Spending time with family and friends
- Taking more vacations
- Sustaining good health
- Protecting retirement savings
- Moving to a warmer climate
- Downsizing house and other assets
- Becoming a mentor to younger people
- Donating time and wealth to philanthropic organizations
- Distributing wealth to family and philanthropic organizations

## Common Risks

At this point in a retiree's life, protecting and preserving retirement savings are of primary importance. Most other financial risks have already been addressed. Having an estate plan and adequate life, health, and long-term care insurance is of primary importance. Depending on the situation, life insurance may not be important. The purpose of life insurance is to protect those who rely on your income and to offset any potential estate taxes. The common financial risks confronting this group include the following:

- Spending more than what is appropriate
- Failing to adjust a financial plan as needed
- Carrying too little or too much insurance
- Failing to update wills and trusts
- Being too conservative so that their portfolios do not outpace inflation
- Paying more than their fair share of estate taxes due to lack of planning

# Common Objectives

## *Portfolio Return Aspiration*

Given the varying time horizons, retirees should strike a balance between equities and fixed-income. Those with longer time horizons should allocate a greater amount to equities whereas those with shorter time horizons should allocate more to fixed-income. The risk profile of the investor also plays a significant role in the asset allocation and thus the expected portfolio return. Matching expected return with anticipated financial obligations is a smart move.

## *Risk Tolerance*

Given a more modest time horizon and relatively low noninvestment income, retirees typically have a lower capacity for risk than both early accumulators and mid-life consolidators. As a result, their risk profile tends to be low to moderate. People with higher levels of wealth will naturally have a higher capacity for risk. However, their tolerance and/or need may dictate a conservative to moderate portfolio. Remember that although you may have the tolerance and capacity for risk, you may not have the need. Taking more risk with no need for additional reward and benefit is simply poor decision making.

# Common Constraints

## *Time Horizon*

The time horizon for retirees can vary substantially and depends on their investment stage at retirement. A portfolio may be managed with a somewhat different time horizon to accommodate either the gifting of assets to heirs or the gifting of assets to charities, which tend to have long-term time horizons. Time horizons for retirees can range anywhere from a couple of years to 20 years and beyond.

### Income and Liquidity Needs

People in the spending life-cycle phase have a moderate to high need for liquidity since their spending usually exceeds their noninvestment income. For those who want to gift a significant portion of their assets, they have a lower need for liquidity, and the need for allocation to higher income-generating assets is low.

### Tax Considerations

Tax management is very important for retirees. The number and complexity of tax considerations begin to increase in this phase. Although retirees need to balance taxes on capital gains and income from dividends and interest, they also need to focus on estate tax-planning issues, tax-exempt investments, and trust-planning considerations.

### Legal and Regulatory Considerations

The most common legal and regulatory issues experienced by retirees are those regarding distributions from retirement plans and those related to distributions from estates to heirs and charities.

### Unique Circumstances and Preferences

There are numerous unique circumstances and preferences for retirees that could have an impact on determining and managing their asset allocation. Examples of the most common include prolonged sickness with resulting medical expenses, disability with loss of earned income, and sale of a family business resulting in extra money to invest.

## Optimal Asset Allocations

The optimal mix of assets for retirees emphasizes a balance between equity and fixed-income assets. For those investors with either longer time horizons or greater risk capacity, a portfolio with more equities may be prudent. Enhancing the risk-and-return trade-off profile should be of primary concern and can be accomplished by adding value stocks, small- and micro-cap stocks and real estate investment trusts. In addition, the fixed-income allocation should be composed of U.S. corporate bonds, high-yield bonds, and both international developed fixed-income and international emerging markets fixed-income. As mentioned previously, a U.S. total stock market index fund—preferably an exchange-traded fund—is an ideal primary equity allocation. Exchange-traded funds offer low cost, ease of use, significant availability, maximum liquidity, and, best of all, high diversification.

Investing in a real estate investment trust is a good way to add real estate exposure at a low cost. A cash allocation is highly encouraged as well.

# Model Portfolios

## *Broad Asset Allocation Models*

Figure 13-1 illustrates three broad asset allocation models for retired spenders and gifters. Each broad category is defined by the risk profile for a retiree, which includes conservative, moderate, and aggressive. As you can see, conservative investors should consider allocating about 25 percent to equities, 40 percent to fixed-income, 30 percent to cash and equivalents, and 5 percent to alternative assets. Retirees with the capacity, tolerance, and need for aggressive investing should consider allocating about 50 percent of their portfolio to equities, about 30 percent to fixed-income, and 10 percent to cash and equivalents. The remaining 10 percent should be invested in alternative assets, principally real estate although a case can be made for commodities or other precious or collectible assets.

| Asset Class | Conservative Investors | Moderate Investors | Aggressive Investors |
|---|---|---|---|
| Equities | 25% | 40% | 50% |
| Fixed-Income | 40% | 35% | 30% |
| Cash & Equivalents | 30% | 20% | 10% |
| Alternative Assets | 5% | 5% | 10% |

Figure 13-1    **Broad Asset Allocation Model Portfolios**

| Asset Class | Allocation and Index Fund |
|---|---|
| **EQUITIES:** | **25 - 50%** |
| Total U.S. Stock Market | iShares Total U.S. Stock Market-IYY |
| Small Cap Value | iShares S&P SmallCap 600 Value-IJS |
| Micro-Cap | iShares Russell MicroCap-IWC |
| International | iShares MSCI EAFE-EFA |
| **FIXED-INCOME:** | **30 - 40%** |
| Total U.S. Bond Market | iShares Lehman Aggregate Bond Fund-AGG |
| High-Yield Bonds | Vanguard High-Yield Corporate-VWEHX |
| International Bonds | DFA Five-Year Global Fixed-Income-DFGBX |
| **CASH & EQUIVALENTS:** | **10 - 30%** |
| Money Markets | Treasury bills, savings or certificates of deposit |
| **ALTERNATIVES:** | **5 - 10%** |
| Real Estate | Cohen & Steers Realty Majors-ICF |

**Figure 13-2    Specific Asset Class Model Portfolios**

## Specific Asset Class Models

Figure 13-2 shows what individual assets you should consider for your portfolio. This figure reiterates the ideal allocation ranges for the primary asset classes with exchanged-traded index funds.

Evaluate the model portfolio and exchange-traded funds within the context that best serves your situation, circumstances, and objectives. It might be a good idea to hire a professional financial advisor. For more help on how best to evaluate and select a financial advisor, read Chapter 16. This chapter also provides suggestions for recommended books to read, Web sites to visit, and publications to peruse.

The portfolios in Figure 13-2 should be considered benchmarks by which to compare your present and anticipated asset allocation. For best results, modify the chart according to your unique personal financial situation.

# A Review

The main concern facing retirees is two-fold. The first is having a portfolio large enough to fund future financial obligations, and the second is to have sufficient liquidity and current income for immediate needs and the distribution of assets to heirs and charities. Given the need for greater liquidity and current income, retirees should consider allocating some of their portfolio out of equities and into fixed-income and cash. Consequently, the portfolio will shift from being growth-oriented to being income-oriented.

Although retirees have varied time horizons, most time horizons can be considered moderate. Because most retirees have a lower capacity for risk, fixed-income and cash investments should be the primary asset class. However, for those retirees who will gift assets to heirs and charities, a long-term time horizon approach should be employed to adequately manage the assets to be gifted.

As with all investors, regardless of life cycle, portfolio reoptimization is key to maintaining an optimal portfolio, or one best positioned to achieve your goals and objectives. Reoptimization includes reevaluating your present financial plan, rebalancing your asset mix, reallocating savings contributions, and relocating specific investments. Given that an investor's portfolio will change over time, reoptimization is highly desirable. Also, your financial plan should change over time as will your financial position, goals and objectives, and your risk profile. Adapting to personal and portfolio changes over time is highly important and critical for long-term financial success.

---

In the next chapter, you will learn about the leading misconceptions of asset allocation and some of the common mistakes investors make when employing asset allocation.

# PART FOUR

# FINAL WORD ON WHAT YOU NEED TO KNOW

# 14

# Common Mistakes and Behavioral Blunders: Avoid Sabotaging Your Asset Allocation

## Common Mistakes of Asset Allocation

Smart people make dumb mistakes all the time. Allocating and managing portfolios successfully in today's marketplace is difficult. There are many pitfalls along the way to complicate matters. When investors and portfolio managers fail to avoid mistakes, they place portfolios at risk. At stake are not only the growth and safety of investors' portfolios but also their future financial independence, control, and security. As a result, investors and financial professionals need to be aware of the common mistakes that can be made when employing asset allocation so that they can avoid them. Do not sabotage your asset allocation and therefore self-implode your portfolio.

This chapter discusses 17 common mistakes that can be made when using asset allocation and helpful hints as to how to avoid making them.

## Failing to Set SMART Financial Goals

You cannot hit a target you are not aiming for. Investors need to do a fair degree of preparation. Unfortunately, a large number of investors manage their portfolios in a haphazard, sporadic, and ineffective manner. Often they fail to set financial goals, which is a basic tenet of investing. Without a solid understanding of your specific goals and investment needs, you will be unable to design or manage your portfolio properly. An accurate assessment of specific goals and needs is essential in order to establish the right mix and specific allocations of asset classes. Your goals and needs are the driving force upon which your portfolio is built.

Determining specific goals and needs is only half the job. The other half is ensuring they are realistic, achievable, measurable, acceptable, and for a set period of time. As we all know, many investors have unrealistic goals, and these sometimes translate into portfolios that are unsuitable or inappropriate. Unsuitable portfolios will surely not achieve your financial goals and objectives. Make every effort to establish SMART financial goals and think in terms of accomplishing them when making each one of your investment decisions.

## Discounting the Trade-off of Risk and Return

Building a portfolio and then managing that portfolio according to the risk-and-return trade-off profile is central to gaining and maintaining a performance edge. Without adhering to this rule, you place your portfolio on shaky ground and potentially set yourself up for the harsh reality of either underperformance due to taking too little risk or sharp portfolio declines from assuming greater risk than justified. By thinking in terms of the risk-and-return trade-off profile rather than discounting its importance, you position your portfolio to earn the returns you need, thereby accomplishing your SMART financial goals. Remember, risk and return are explicitly linked, and no optimal portfolio can be built without putting this concept to work.

## Having Unrealistic Return Expectations

Every investor hears plenty of investment and performance "noise." Investors are frequently bombarded with enticing offerings and words of praise about new and better investment products that deliver stellar performances. Perhaps you have even heard your friends or family members talk about how well their investments are doing compared to yours. This is plain and simple noise that can only hurt your approach to investing.

One of the most difficult and subjective tasks associated with investing is having realistic expectations. Investors need to exercise significant discretion and resist sabotaging their portfolios simply because of what everyone else is doing or is earning on their investments.

Your asset mix should remain constant, and modifications should only be made when you experience material life changes. Switching from asset class to asset class in the hopes of earning a higher return hardly ever works out and could spell disaster. You could miss out on nice gains in the asset classes you switched out of, or experience a significant loss from having too much in an asset class you emphasized. The best way to manage your assets is to have a steady and consistent asset mix that is developed with realistic expectations and modified only by a judicious reevaluation of your goals, needs, and risk profile.

## Misinterpreting Risk Tolerance

Many investors confuse risk tolerance with risk capacity and vice versa. Your risk tolerance is your willingness to assume risk in order to earn the return you need. Misinterpreting risk tolerance may result in a portfolio that inherently has more risk than appropriate or one where the returns will be less than needed because it was designed to maximize returns with a lower risk tolerance. A well-designed risk tolerance questionnaire together with a face-to-face meeting is a prudent approach to identifying your tolerance for risk.

## Misjudging Risk Capacity

Don't invest what you can't afford to lose. This wisdom gets at the heart of addressing your risk capacity when investing. Risk capacity is your ability to assume risk. An investor's *capacity* for risk is not determined by or affected by his or her *tolerance* for risk. The two are completely different.

Some investors do not take into account their capacity to assume risk. Unfortunately, their tolerance for risk often masters their capacity for risk. Remember to always think in terms of your capacity for risk taking. Don't let your emotions get the best of you so that you would invest more than you can afford to lose.

## Disregarding Risk Need

From time to time you have seen investors assume more risk than was necessary. Regardless of your tolerance and capacity for risk, if you do not need to assume additional risk, then why do so? Investors who have accumulated the assets that will be required to fund their future financial obligations and needs should not take on any more risk than they need to. By doing so, investors place their portfolios at risk for performance they have no need for.

Many times investors will invest their assets at risk levels higher than necessary because that is what they have been doing most of their lives.

You must put a stop to your level of portfolio risk when you have no *need* for risk even though you could *tolerate* more. Regardless of high levels of risk capacity and risk tolerance, wise investors know this and assume only the risk that is justified. As an investor, you should evaluate your financial position and determine what your need for risk truly is. Building your portfolio based on that need for risk is ideal.

### Underestimating Time Horizon

Your time horizon is the period from the present to a future point in time when you will no longer need the assets in your portfolio. Many investors mistakenly believe their time horizon is from the present to the day they plan to retire. Unfortunately, that could not be farther from the truth. At retirement, it is not their time horizon that may change, but rather their risk tolerance and liquidity needs.

Portfolios based on shorter time horizons will be overallocated to fixed-income assets and possibly underperform as a result. Life-changing events, such as retirement, are taken into consideration through asset allocation modifications. Your time horizon typically extends well into your retirement. Once you retire, you can alter your asset allocation, but prior to that point it is wise to have a well-diversified and allocated portfolio that uses an appropriate time horizon.

### Miscalculating Liquidity Needs

Underestimating how much liquidity you will need could create a situation where a portion of your portfolio may need to be reallocated to meet the liquidity need. This may involve allocating out of growth-oriented investments and income-oriented investments or simply selling assets altogether. Both result in additional and unnecessary transaction costs and tax consequences. Better to plan in advance for such a scenario so that you are not taken by surprise.

### Overlooking Special Circumstances

Similar to investments, investors have different interests or limitations that can sometimes change the way a portfolio is designed or managed. Some investors like to invest using a socially responsible approach. Others may prefer not to invest globally, while still other investors may be unable to invest in certain industries or investments because of legal or ethical constraints. As a result, it is prudent to identify any unique circumstances and preferences that could be considered material and incorporate them into your investing.

## Ignoring Inflation

Over time inflation can erode the real value of a portfolio, thus depriving the investor of real returns. Portfolios with greater allocations to fixed-income and cash and equivalents are more susceptible to this type of risk since returns tend to be lower. Once taxes on earnings are taken into account, the real return from fixed-income investments is even lower. Your target should be to earn a return that outpaces inflation and the impact of taxes.

As a general rule, the longer your investment time horizon, the more you should allocate to equity investments. Conversely, for shorter investment time horizons, the more you should allocate to fixed-income and cash and equivalents investments. The allocation to equity investments and time horizon are thus highly correlated.

## Excluding Desirable Asset Classes

Research studies have concluded that *how* you allocate a portfolio, rather than *which* investments you select or *when* you buy or sell them, is the leading determinant of investment performance over time. As a result, make every effort to allocate a portfolio among all appropriate asset classes. Each asset class and asset subclass provides return enhancing and risk reducing benefits. By not incorporating appropriate classes, a portfolio may not exhibit the desired risk-and-return trade-off profile.

Regardless of your risk tolerance, you should want to earn a return that outpaces inflation and taxes over time. Some investors shy away from moderately risky assets, such as large-cap equities, fearing the market's ups and downs will hinder long-term performance. By doing so, investors may find it very difficult, if not impossible, to fund the style of living they desire in retirement. Even conservative investors with a long-term time horizon are highly encouraged to consider a small allocation to equities for their portfolio, thus increasing the odds that its performance will outpace that of inflation and taxes.

## Selecting and Holding Improper Allocations

By selecting inappropriate asset class weightings, a portfolio will exhibit a risk-and-return trade-off profile that is inconsistent with an investor's objectives and constraints. As a result, the portfolio may earn a lower return than expected or experience greater risk than anticipated. Be careful not to over- or underweight any asset class, thus maximizing a portfolio's risk-and-return trade-off profile within the context of your objectives and constraints.

## Confusing Asset Allocation with Diversification

Many investors confuse asset allocation with diversification. They believe the two are the same thing. For many investors, this confusion is not their mistake. Many money management companies, financial authors, and investment professionals explain it this way because some of them do not fully understand the difference. This confusion is one of the leading misconceptions of asset allocation.

Diversification impacts only the management of risk, specifically the reduction of investment-specific risk. On the other hand, asset allocation not only maximizes risk-adjusted return but also reduces risk by combining asset classes that have less than perfect correlations. Asset allocation addresses both the numerator and denominator of the risk and return trade-off equation while diversification deals only with the numerator: risk management.

## Overestimating the Level of Diversification

Diversification is the key to reducing risk, namely investment-specific risk. There are two ways to overestimate the level of diversification. First, one may believe that the quantity of securities currently in a portfolio is sufficient to create a diversified portfolio when, in fact, it is not. Diversifying using individual securities typically requires about 15 securities before the optimal diversification level is reached. Each security added before 15 provides a risk-reducing benefit, but adding more than 15 usually does not provide much benefit as the level of diversification is at or near the maximum point.

Second, but much less important, although a portfolio may hold an appropriate quantity of securities, the majority of the securities may be too similar to provide significant diversification benefits. For example, the stocks of General Motors and Ford will provide some diversification benefits, but due to their inherent industry similarities, holding both in a portfolio will not provide a significant level of diversification. Diversifying across fundamentally different sectors or industries is therefore recommended.

## Failing to Balance Investment and Tax Matters

Taxes can be a significant detriment to portfolio performance and an investor's financial independence, security, and control. Given the complexities and magnitude of tax considerations from investor to investor, it is appropriate to not only incorporate all relevant considerations at the onset when designing portfolios but also to address them on a continuing basis when managing portfolios. The primary tax considerations include capital gains, ordinary income, and estate related.

Investors frequently let the impact of taxes impede their decisions to sell investments. It is true that tax consequences can and sometimes do significantly impact returns. However, investors need to base their decisions on whether or not an investment is suitable and appropriate. On the other hand, there are a number of investors who place too little emphasis on the impact of taxes. In summary, investors should balance tax and investment considerations, and remember that suitability and appropriateness of an investment take precedence over tax consequences. Never hold an inappropriate investment.

## Paying Excessive Portfolio Expenses

If you don't keep it, did you really make it? That is one of my favorite quotes relating to investment performance. Take a moment and think about it and how it applies to your portfolio.

Over time, the compounding effect of portfolio management expenses can be quite large and surprising, thus depriving a portfolio of returns. Even small annual expenses can add up to significant expenses over the long term. Obviously it is more or less impossible not to pay some sort of portfolio-related expenses. Nevertheless, you should focus on minimizing portfolio management expenses, namely trading costs, both commissions and bid-ask spreads, and investment advisory fees. There are a significant number of investment advisors who would be glad to have your business. With all of the competition and the breadth and depth of advisor opportunities, do not condone high portfolio expenses. Ask for lower fees and commissions or switch to another advisor.

## Neglecting Portfolio Reoptimization

The purpose of reoptimizing is to keep your portfolio's risk-and-return profile in an acceptable range. Reoptimizing includes reevaluating, rebalancing, reallocating, and relocating. These are the four Rs of reoptimization. By not reoptimizing, investors can expose their portfolio to greater risk than appropriate or less risk than needed to earn a desired rate of return.

Rebalancing too infrequently may alter a portfolio's risk-and-return trade-off profile to one that is inappropriate for an investor's objectives and constraints. The less frequently you monitor and rebalance, the greater the opportunity for asset classes to move undetected outside of allocation ranges. As a result, a portfolio's optimal risk-and-return trade-off profile will change.

On the other hand, an investor may rebalance too frequently. Doing so can expose an investor to higher transaction costs and capital gains taxes than is appropriate under normal circumstances. In addition, there is the additional time commitment that is needed to rebalance more frequently. As the old saying goes, "Time is money."

A final word of caution: Be aware of the total costs when rebalancing. By underestimating rebalancing costs, an investor will either not initiate an otherwise prudent rebalancing action or prompt a rebalancing action that is unnecessary. A solid grasp of all rebalancing costs is needed to ensure that suitable rebalancing is carried out with the minimum of costs.

## Beware of Behavioral Blunders

We are all human and humans make behavioral blunders all the time, particularly when investing. Make no mistake about it. Your behavior is a primary influence on the success or failure of you as an investor and on your investing. Yes, we all know better, but somehow, sometimes, someplace, we still find ways to sabotage things—or in this case, our asset allocations. In order to become better investors, people first need to realize and understand what behavioral blunders they may be making or are tempted by. Thereafter investors will need stern resolve to ensure they do not get entangled and commit these potentially costly blunders. With investing, remember to always focus on what you can control. Your behavior is definitely part of what you can control.

Many behavioral blunders that investors make are the result of bad or misleading advice that has the single goal of playing on their fears and desires. Unfortunately, many investors are attracted to bad advice simply because of the way it is presented and because of what it promises. Sometimes the flashy yet bad product sells over the boring but effective product. That's just the way things seem to be at times.

Do you think the investment industry is any different? Think again. Investment companies are constantly advertising products or services that motivate investors to make rash and emotional decisions. Often bad decisions. Remaining in control and using common sense is your best defense.

## Behavioral Finance Explained

Behavioral finance is the study of the what, when, where, and how of investor decision making, emotional influences, and persistent biases. The field of behavioral finance is relatively young, with solid research forthcoming over the last couple of decades. The goal of behavioral finance is to enhance rational investor decision making by understanding irrational behavior, appreciating the consequences, and finding ways to avoid this behavior through rational decision-making approaches.

Some of the inherent factors that influence investor behavior include preferences, intuition, character, uncertainty, beliefs, values, attitude, perception, emotions, judgment, probability, and simple mental stability. Furthermore, these factors can be genetic or learned, conscious or unconscious, and with varying levels of conviction. Investors are all different as is their behavior.

Making decisions as prudent, rational, and informed investors is the best way to investment success. Unfortunately, many investors do not exercise this behavior and therefore place their investing at risk. Much research has been done regarding behavioral finance and the vast majority of the results point to common errors from irrational behavior. Worse yet, this research has shown these errors to be predictable, consistent, and pervasive.

## Impact of Behavioral Blunders

Behavioral blunders can have a profound and long-term impact on portfolio performance and overall investing success. When investment results are not as expected, many investors blame the investment plan, the portfolio allocation, and many times the financial markets. Nothing could be farther from the truth. Research has found that the primary culprit of investment failure is the behavior of investors and how that impacts their decisions. Not the plan, not the allocation, and not the financial markets. Given this and given that proper asset allocation depends on rational behavior, it is vitally important to learn about the potential pitfalls so you can avoid them..

## Select Behavioral Blunders

Behavioral blunders can occur during the investment planning phase, the investment implementation phase, or the investment management phase.

### Investment Planning Phase

The following are only a few of the behavioral blunders that investors can make during the investment planning phase. There are many, many more. These behavioral blunders occur in thought rather than in action.

- *Overconfident*: Behavior where investors think they are much smarter than other investors and therefore believe they can earn superior results consistently over time.

- *Overly optimistic*: Behavior where investors think the financial markets pose no great risk or danger and therefore they typically assume more risk than necessary.
- *Stereotyping*: Behavior where investors think all investments in a certain asset class, all returns over a certain period of time, or all financial markets during a certain time are the same.
- *Mental Accounting*: Behavior where investors think that the individual components making up a portfolio are more important than the portfolio as a whole. Compartmentalizing their decisions is often the result of such behavior.
- *Anchoring*: Behavior where investors become engrossed and hooked on a specific investment, asset class, purchase price, or selling price.
- *Representativeness*: Behavior where investors draw a conclusion based on what they know and are comfortable with their conclusion rather than what is really happening.
- *Blinders*: Behavior where investors, either consciously or subconsciously, ignore material changes or events surrounding an investment to maintain stability and comfort.

## Investment Implementation Phase

The following behavioral blunders deal with specific actions rather than with thought. Similar to the blunders listed above, these are a select number of behavioral blunders that investors can make during the investment implementation phase.

- *Crowd Instinct*: Behavior where investors do what other investors are doing regardless of the risk-and-return possibilities. Chasing hot stocks is one example.
- *Action Avoidance*: Behavior where investors refrain from taking investment action for any number of reasons. Fear of the market is one example.
- *Loss Aversion*: Behavior where investors do not act to stem losses simply because the pain experienced from previous similar actions was substantial.

## Investment Managing Phase

Now that we have discussed both investment planning and investment implementation behavioral blunders, we next mention some of the blunders investors may make during the investment managing phase. The focus again shifts to specific thoughts rather than specific actions.

- *Denial*: Behavior where investors do not admit to their mistakes and therefore pursue a path of denials having made a certain investment decision. Denying allocating 50 percent of a portfolio to a stock that declined 25 percent in one day is an example of denial.
- *Regret*: Behavior where investors regret having made certain investment decisions given the outcome of the results. Regretting buying based on a rumor is an example.
- *Hindsight Error*: Behavior where investors overemphasize the reason a certain result occurred and apply that thought to future decisions. Thinking an investment was successful because it was purchased before stellar earnings were released and applying that to the next investment decision is an example of hindsight error.
- *Result Rationalizing*: Behavior where investors settle on factors that were not the primary cause of a certain investment result. Thinking that market fundamentals are the sole cause of a portfolio that declines sharply rather than the real cause—poor asset allocation—is one example of result rationalizing.
- *Selective Memory*: Behavior where investors tend to remember only what they want to remember, usually the good over the bad. Future actions without knowing the complete picture could then occur.

Making investment decisions as a rational and prudent investor is the key for proper asset allocation. By repeatedly committing one or more behavioral mistakes, investors can prove to be their own worst enemy. At risk is the chance you may sabotage your asset allocation and place your portfolio in danger. Even what may seem like meaningless missteps can have a drastic impact on your investment performance over time. Let steadfast discipline and objective thinking be your foundation for future investment decisions.

---

In the next chapter, you will learn about the leading misconceptions of asset allocation and how to separate fact from fiction.

# 15

# Leading Misconceptions: Separating Fact from Fiction

## Leading Misconceptions of Asset Allocation

Is it fact or fiction? Now that we have discussed what asset allocation is, we turn our attention to what asset allocation is not. Unfortunately, there are a fair number of misconceptions about asset allocation in the marketplace. Compounding the problem is that few experts in the field– both practitioners and those in academia—spend ample time and resources to research asset allocation. Given the glamour of stock picking and day trading, significantly more work has been concentrated on those areas. Fortunately, more and more books such as this one are dissecting asset allocation and taking on the challenge of separating fact from fiction.

The following misconceptions were derived through extensive research and over a decade of hands-on experience with investors and the investing public at large. There is no particular order to those listed. It is very important

that you become familiar with these leading misconceptions of asset allocation so your investing can be based on facts.

## Myth: Asset Allocation Is the Same as Diversification

Not only is this a leading misconception of asset allocation, but it is *the* top
misconception. The first thought that generally comes to mind when one hears
of asset allocation is the concept of diversification. Many people then incorrectly assume that a diversified portfolio is a properly allocated portfolio.

Diversification only impacts the management of risk, specifically the
reduction of investment-specific risk. On the other hand, asset allocation
maximizes the risk-adjusted return, namely the enhancement of return and the
reduction of risk. This is accomplished by combining asset classes that have
less than perfect correlations. Asset allocation impacts both the numerator and
denominator of the risk-and-return trade-off equation whereas diversification
impacts only the numerator.

## Myth: Asset Allocation Is the Same Thing as Multiclass Investing

Although asset allocation and multiclass investing tend to go hand in hand, this
is not always the case. There is a clear distinction, and there are rare cases when
the two differ. Asset allocation is a strategy of how best to maximize return,
whereas multiclass investing is usually the result of such a strategy. Asset allocation does not require that a portfolio be multiclass. In certain, and sometimes
unusual circumstances, asset allocation may call for investing in a single asset
class. This circumstance only happens when an investor either has an incredibly
short-term time horizon or is hyperaggressive. In the latter case, an investor who
needs his or her money within three months for a home purchase, for example,
should only consider cash and equivalents investments. Doing so will protect the
hyperaggressive investor's money and ensure it is available when needed.

## Myth: Mutual Funds Constitute a Properly Allocated Portfolio

Much the same as asset allocation and diversification, mutual funds do not
always constitute a properly allocated portfolio. Again, asset allocation is
an investment strategy while mutual funds are the vehicle for implementing that strategy. Some mutual funds, such as balanced mutual funds and
asset allocation mutual funds, can be classified as multiclass portfolios, but
that does not always mean they are properly allocated. In addition, owning
one mutual fund does not guarantee that your portfolio is diversified either.
However, depending on your investment objective and time horizon, you
might allocate your portfolio to a mutual fund that holds growth stocks,

value stocks, and short-term and long-term fixed-income securities. In this case, your portfolio may be close to being properly allocated. Determine your optimal asset mix first and then consider using appropriate mutual funds to develop the asset classes you wish to hold.

## Myth: Asset Allocation Is a Buy-and-Hold Strategy

Try not to confuse asset allocation with the philosophy of buy and hold. Under the buy-and-hold philosophy, a portfolio is created and little to no revisions are made to the asset mix. Over time, price changes will alter—sometimes substantially—the portfolio's asset mix. In consequence, you will have a portfolio that either exhibits greater risk than appropriate since the portfolio is overallocated to one or more asset classes or experiences a lower actual total return than expected. The latter is the result of the portfolio not receiving the return enhancing benefits derived from rotating price leadership and rebalancing. Nevertheless, in neither of the two aforementioned cases will a portfolio remain optimal for very long after constructed. Lastly and very importantly, under a buy-and-hold philosophy, market weakness will have a magnified impact since some asset classes will be disproportionately large if not rebalanced. Thus, severe weakness impacting the large, and arguably overvalued, asset class will have a drastic negative impact on your portfolio value and resulting portfolio performance.

## Myth: Asset Allocation Is Only for Conservative Investors

Asset allocation is a prudent strategy for all types of investors, regardless of risk tolerance. It is true that asset allocation is more beneficial for conservative to moderate investors; however, even high-risk tolerant investors can benefit from its application. As mentioned previously, asset allocation does not require multiclass investing, only that the risk tolerance of the investor is aligned with the asset classes employed. Consequently, high-risk tolerant investors will not be hindered by its application. An investor with a high-risk tolerance could build a high-risk portfolio by allocating to one or more highly correlated high-risk asset classes, such as small-cap and mid-cap growth. By doing so, an investor will achieve his or her goal of building a high-risk portfolio, but at the same time enhance the risk-and-return trade-off profile. Asset allocation is quite flexible in this regard.

## Myth: Asset Allocation Cannot Be Combined with Security Selection and Market Timing

Not true. As a matter of fact, many financial advisors incorporate all three strategies into their management practices. Each strategy can be fully utilized to build a portfolio through a process-oriented approach. For example, when building a portfolio, a financial advisor can first establish the optimal asset mix, thus utilizing asset allocation, and then select the appropriate investments via security selection. Each security selected can fully accommodate the optimal asset mix, whether it be equities, fixed-income, alternative, and/or cash and equivalents. Finally, once the optimal asset mix is established and the individual securities are selected, the financial advisor can then determine the right time or price to make the investment, thus utilizing the strategy of market timing. The important point to remember is that asset allocation must be established first, followed by security selection, then followed by market timing. This process cannot be accomplished in reverse order.

## Myth: Allocating 100 percent to a Conservative Asset Class Creates a Conservative Portfolio

Investing solely in blue chip stocks or an otherwise conservative asset class will not necessarily create an overall conservative portfolio. Rather, allocating to only one asset class or investment type will actually increase your risk, sometimes substantially. To create a conservative portfolio, you need to allocate to a multiple of asset classes. One simply is not enough for conservative risk tolerant investors. Allocating to both small-cap stocks and large-cap blue chip stocks will decrease portfolio volatility and enhance the risk-adjusted return. Remember that multiclass portfolios are normally much less risky than single-class portfolios.

## Myth: Asset Allocations Are Relatively Consistent from Investor to Investor

Depending on one's risk tolerance and time horizon, asset allocations can differ, and sometimes drastically, from investor to investor. For instance, allocations to equity investments and fixed-income investments are much different for conservative investors than they are for aggressive investors. Not only may allocations to certain asset classes differ but so can the asset classes employed. Aggressive investors will tend to allocate to more risky assets whereas conservative investors will tend to allocate to less risky asset classes. Thus, the breadth and depth of the allocations *do* differ from investor to investor.

## Myth: Investment Time Horizon Extends until Retirement

Investors believe their time horizon lasts until they retire rather than until they no longer need the assets in their portfolios. Although many investors do understand that their time horizons do extend well into their retirement, the result of believing otherwise can be rather severe. At stake is your ability to earn suitable returns after retirement to help fund your retirement and your desired standard of living. By misallocating a portfolio at retirement, an investor may possess a portfolio that is overallocated to fixed-income and possibly cash and equivalents. As a result, that particular investor's portfolio performance may not be adequate to provide income in the future. Protect your future financial security and incorporate the appropriate investment time horizon.

## Myth: Tactical Asset Allocation Is a True Asset Allocation Strategy

Tactical asset allocation is *not* a true asset allocation strategy, but rather a glamorous name for market timing. Although tactical asset allocation does adopt some of the cornerstone principles of asset allocation, it also places too much emphasis on profiting from short-term price movements to constitute a true asset allocation strategy. Not all tactical asset allocation strategies employed by professional money managers are the same. Some emphasize market timing more than others. One professional money manager may alter the allocations in a portfolio up to 50 percent of the portfolio, while another may only alter about 10 percent of a portfolio's allocations. The degree of emphasis depends on the preferences of the money manager and the investor.

*Market timing* is a term most appropriately used in the context of altering individual holdings whereas *tactical asset allocation* is synonymous with altering allocations where individual holdings are an afterthought.

## Myth: Optimal Asset Mix Should Change
## with Market Advances and Declines

This misconception is quite similar to that of tactical asset allocation being a true asset allocation strategy. True asset allocation does not emphasize the changing of allocations in response to changing market conditions. However, true asset allocation does call for changing allocations in response to either changes to investor-centered factors or changes to market-centered factors. Since allocations are based on certain inputs, changes should be made as appropriate if there are changes to these inputs. Simple market ups and downs should not be considered significant and material, and therefore no allocation changes should be made. As a general rule, if a change or fluctuation is only short term, then no changes to your long-term strategy and optimal asset mix should be made. Conversely, long-term changes should be accounted for with changes to portfolio allocations.

## Myth: Asset Allocation Will Hinder Portfolio Performance

This is another one of the top leading misconceptions and an incredible fabrication of the truth. As mentioned many times throughout this book, numerous landmark research studies have concluded that *how* you allocate your assets, rather than *which* individual investments you select or *when* you buy or sell them, is the primary determinant of portfolio performance over time. As a result, it is imperative that you develop, incorporate, and stick to an intelligent asset allocation policy.

The proper allocation of assets in your portfolio will not hinder portfolio performance in and of itself. Rather, it is how you establish your optimal asset mix and rebalance your portfolio over time that will determine your portfolio performance. Obviously, for you to profit, the assets in your portfolio must be given an opportunity to advance. The surest way to hinder portfolio performance is to rebalance each time an asset class moves higher in price. This is where target allocation ranges are highly ideal. The benefits from target allocation ranges are twofold. First, they allow your assets to benefit from price appreciation, and secondly, they allow for risk control since they trigger rebalancing once allocations become overallocated and arguably more risky for the investor. Given rotating price leadership amount asset classes, without target allocation ranges, the only thing added to your portfolio at the end of the day is volatility—no added portfolio performance. The best method to maximize return potential and minimize risk is to rebalance an asset class to some degree after significant price appreciation. Thus, when an asset class corrects in price, some of the gain will be sitting safely in your portfolio because of your rebalancing efforts.

Aggressive investors can establish wider target allocation ranges to allow for more potential price appreciation and more potential risk, whereas conservative investors can establish smaller target allocation ranges for a less risky portfolio.

Remember that asset allocation does not require you to allocate among all the asset classes. In consequence, if you have a significant risk tolerance, you may have a portfolio with high-risk investments, thus enabling you to outperform the market, or on the flip side, underperform given the heightened risk level.

## Myth: Asset Allocation Adds Unnecessary Trading Costs

Each and every transaction involves costs, regardless of whether you are employing asset allocation, security selection, or market timing. Your goal, however, is to approach investment decisions intelligently and to minimize trading costs. As a result, do not rebalance each time an allocation deviates from the optimal allocation. Doing so will require extensive time and add unnecessary trading costs. The most prudent method is to initiate rebalancing when allocations move outside of established targets, namely allocation floors and ceilings. Depending on your risk tolerance, you can make your target range very small or very wide. More aggressive investors may find it appropriate to establish a wide target range, possibly 10 percent or more on each side of the optimal allocation. For instance, if your optimal allocation for equities is 50 percent, you can set your target allocation range at 40 to 60 percent. Then, as long as the equity allocation remains in this range, no rebalancing needs to be initiated. For conservative investors, a more narrow range such as 3 to 5 percent may be more appropriate. Once allocations move outside the target allocation range, rebalancing is initiated. Doing so will not add unnecessary trading costs; it will actually minimize them.

In summary, rebalancing does add to trading costs, but these added expenses are arguably less than those of security selection and surely lower than that of market timing. Both investment strategies call for a greater number of transactions as compared to asset allocation.

## Immutable Lessons of Asset Allocation

Asset allocation is a very powerful investment strategy and the primary driver of investment performance over time. Although asset allocation cannot specifically determine which investments to select, asset allocation can provide a blueprint for which asset classes and asset subclasses are best for your particular situation. After reading this book, you will undoubtedly see how straightforward and beneficial asset allocation truly is. However, one type of asset allocation is not a perfect fit for all types of investors. Each person's financial situation and personal circumstances is likely to be different and likely to change over time. As a result, it is vitally important that you work diligently to establish your optimal asset allocation, one that will give you the best chances for investment success.

The key to protecting and growing your wealth is to develop a sound investment plan, implement that plan fully, and follow it with strong conviction. Unfortunately, many investors fall prey to their emotions and place their financial independence, control, and security at risk. Make every attempt to avoid this scenario.

In the next chapter, you will learn about the value of professional help and how working with a professional can help to maximize your asset allocation..

# 16

# Professional Advice and Resources: Maximize Your Asset Allocation

## Importance of Professional Advice

This book is intended to give you all of the tools and resources required to easily and successfully design, construct, monitor, and rebalance your optimal portfolio using asset allocation. However, this book is not intended to be a complete substitute for experienced professional assistance and counseling in every situation. In an endeavor as critical as managing your investments, it is prudent to handle some situations with the help of a competent professional advisor. Many individual investors simply do not have the time, patience, or persistence to deal effectively with their investments over the long term. Many investors have the motivation to put in the required time to fully address their investments at the outset, but become less motivated as time goes by. In addition, there are some very common mistakes that individual investors make that a professional advisor can help to overcome. In addition to the most common asset allocation mistakes discussed in the previous chapter, individual investors frequently make the following mistakes as well:

- Make ad hoc fear-based revisions at the first sign of market weakness
- Omit the process of drafting an investment policy statement
- Emphasize individual securities rather than the overall portfolio
- Fail to reevaluate their financial situation at least annually and then revise their investment policy statement
- Get caught up in the hype of the market and lose investment focus
- Chase the latest investment fads

## When to Seek Professional Advice

There will be times when you can handle most of the management of your financial affairs. However, there will be other times when you should seek the help of an investment pro. The list below examines some of the situations when it makes the most sense to seek the help of a competent investment advisor:

- *When you are confronted with complicated financial products and strategies*: Most of us have heard of disability, liability umbrella, and long-term care insurance, but do we really know the basics, let alone what type of coverage to select? People with employment stock options or business owners with limited family partnerships can also benefit from the help of an advisor.
- *When you get married*: Combining your money, and debt, with your spouse can pose significant challenges. These challenges range from deciding to file a joint tax return or single tax returns to taking advantage of all child-related tax benefits. Financial planning advisors and tax advisors may provide you with the best solutions.
- *When buying and selling a house*: Although not their traditional work, financial advisors may provide some much needed insights into such issues as capital gains, down payment, mortgage alternatives, and home sale reinvestment options.
- *When buying or selling a business*: The complexities of buying or selling a business can be quite significant if not downright grueling. A financial advisor will help with capital gains and proper wealth transfer.
- *When (better say if) you get a divorce*: Simply dividing assets could be a cumbersome and very problematic issue. In addition, new financial plans such as wills and insurance policies will probably need to be revised.

- *When you inherit money*: Although coming into a substantial amount of wealth is generally a good thing, people who have little experience managing money may run into challenges. An investment advisor can help you allocate your inheritance to ensure it lasts for a prolonged period of time.
- *When rolling over your 401(k)*: Although this task is not especially difficult, many investors can get tripped up. A financial advisor will ensure that your rollover is not taxed as an early withdrawal.
- *When saving for college*: From my experience, I have noticed that there are many people who do not know how much money they should be saving each year and what the best investment vehicle is. Since tax codes, especially those targeted at saving for college, seem to change each year, working with a financial advisor will prove very beneficial.
- *When planning and managing your retirement*: Planning your retirement is only half the battle. Managing your retirement is just as important. A good financial advisor will create a plan for you that will give you the best chances of achieving the lifestyle you hope to have during retirement. In addition, they can help you to plan out how best to manage your finances when you are enjoying your retirement.
- *When planning for wealth transfer (e.g., estate planning)*: This area can often be the most complex of all financial matters. Aside from deciding who should receive your wealth, you must decide how much they receive and when they receive it. Other issues such as minimizing taxes and dealing with beneficiaries who are minors can become challenging.

## Evaluating Professional Advice

Obtaining professional advice is a significant step and should not be approached lightly. As with investors and their objectives and constraints, professional advisors also differ in their philosophy, processes, services, education, experience, and their ability to add value. Professional advisors work in many fields and hold various titles, such as investment advisor, financial planner, accountant, estate planner, insurance agent, and stockbroker. Over the last few years, most professional advisors have seen their roles expand and now the lines among them have become greatly blurred. Today it is now commonplace to meet an insurance agent who is also registered as an investment advisor or a stockbroker who engages in the practice of estate planning.

With so many potential professional investment advisors to choose from, the process can seem daunting. Remember, not all professional advisors are equal! Some advisors may say the same things as others, but when you investigate further you will discover significant differences. The following are 11 questions you should investigate when evaluating a potential financial advisor.

## *Question 1: What financial services do the advisors offer?*

It is important to first determine what services you are seeking: investment counseling, total financial planning, estate planning, and/or tax preparation. When you know that, you should investigate whether or not the advisors offer these services. This is important because most professional advisors do not offer a complete array of services. It is common for advisors either to have relationships with outside advisors who can address the areas not serviced or, if their firm is large enough, to have someone else in their firm handle separate services.

## *Question 2: Do the advisors offer customized portfolio solutions or more of a cookie cutter solution?*

Regardless of your financial objectives and constraints, some financial advisors only offer one or two approaches to managing wealth, specifically portfolio management. For instance, you may find advisors who build practically the same portfolio for all of their investors without taking into consideration their ability or willingness to tolerate risk. Most financial advisors realize that customized portfolios provide the best way to achieve investors' goals and objectives. However, be cautious and ask how tailored their portfolio solutions are.

## *Question 3: What are the specific qualifications of the advisors?*

What education do the investment advisors have? Bachelor's? Master's? Find out what their degree is in: finance, accounting, marketing, economics, literature? You would be surprised at the number of advisors I have met who have either no bachelor's degree or a degree in a field unrelated to finance and investing. You should also investigate whether or not the advisors have earned professional designations, such as CPA (Certified Public Accountant), CFP (Certified Financial Planner), CFA (Chartered Financial Analyst), or ChFC (Chartered Financial Consultant). Having a designation illustrates commitment and very specialized knowledge that can separate the top advisors from the rest of the pack.

## *Question 4: How much and of what type of experience do the advisors have?*

You should find out how long the advisors have been in practice and how long they have been in their present role. A follow-up question could address the advisors' specific work experience. Also, do not be fooled by age. I have known many advisors who entered the business late in their careers and consequently had as much (or as little) to offer as someone straight out of college.

## Question 5: How ethical and trustworthy are the advisors?

This question is obviously very subjective and not always easy to answer when you first meet potential advisors. A good way to approach this question is to investigate their backgrounds, specifically whether a regulatory organization or private association to which they belong has publicly disciplined them. To check on an advisor's regulatory records, you should contact the NASD (National Association of Securities Dealers) or any association the advisor may be a member of, such as the Certified Financial Planning Board of Standards (www.CFP.net) or the CFA Institute (www.CFAInstitute.org).

## Question 6: What are the advisors' investment process and investment philosophy?

You would be amazed at the number of advisors who wing it when designing portfolios because they either have no philosophy or fail to adopt one. You should ensure that advisors you are considering incorporate asset allocation into their investment philosophy and apply it to their portfolio management process. Also, you should consider investigating whether or not advisors adopt some sort of plan for building an optimal portfolio. Asking questions at this point is very wise and will minimize issues going forward.

## Question 7: What is the advisors' tax management philosophy?

Advisors approach the tax management issue from different viewpoints. Some advisors underemphasize tax management while others overemphasize it. Specifically, ask about the general degree of turnover, how they incorporate tax management into the rebalancing phase, whether or not they can incorporate tax losses or gains generated outside of the portfolio, and how they approach the issues of loss-harvesting and exchange strategies.

## Question 8: What are the fees and by what method are the advisors paid?

There are many ways an advisor can be compensated: commission, a percentage of a portfolio's market value (asset-sized fee), hourly fees, fees for individual services performed, or any combination. There is no right or wrong fee structure. The best fee structure is what makes sense and is the best fit for you. Personally, I recommend that investors seek advisors with asset-sized fees. With this scenario, a typical investor will pay anywhere from ½ percent to 1½ percent of their portfolio market value in fees to the advisor. This structure is appealing because it motivates the advisor to grow your portfolio, thereby growing his or her fees at the same time. Essentially, one can say that an asset-sized fee structure aligns your interests with the interests of your advisor. Most advisors will be able to provide the investor with a written document outlining their fees. If an advisor cannot provide this, move on. Don't be afraid to ask about fees up front.

## Question 9: What is the long-term performance or track record of the advisors?

The vast majority of advisors can provide you with some sort of performance composite for you to review. When reviewing performance information, be sure to learn which benchmark(s) are employed (such as the S&P 500), how well the advisor performed against the benchmark(s), the consistency of performance over long periods of time, the volatility of performance [especially in relation to the benchmark(s)], the growth of assets under management, and the statement of whether or not the performance conforms to CFA Institute standards. If any of these items are not voluntarily provided, ask the advisor to provide them. If the performance was not created according to CFA Institute standards, ask why. Performance is suspect when the advisor has not conformed to any standards, especially the tough CFA Institute standards. The CFA Institute is the organization that oversees the Chartered Financial Analyst (CFA) designation.

## Question 10: What is the profile of their typical investor?

Your goal here is to find out whether or not the advisor under investigation is knowledgeable about your objectives, constraints, problems, and solutions. Some advisors work with everyone, thus are jacks-of-all-trades, whereas others work only with specialized groups of people, such as affluent investors; thus they are exposed day in and day out to the issues faced by that group and how best to deliver a targeted solution.

Knowing the typical clientele gives you a good idea of the type of problems and solutions the advisor is most experienced with. Since some people require very specific financial solutions, knowing the typical investor will help you to discover whether or not that advisor can effectively work with you.

## Question 11: Is there a personality fit?

The last question deals with whether or not you can work with the advisor. This question is more intuitive-oriented rather than objective-oriented. Usually after the first meeting you will know if there is a fit or not. Is the advisor more serious or humorous? Is the advisor intense or low-key? Is the advisor more professional or down-to-earth? Does he or she play golf? Did a friend refer you? Are your interests similar? Questions like these will help you determine if your personalities mesh, which makes dealing with each other so much easier.

In addition to the questions presented, another good way to evaluate an investment advisor is to review what is called Form ADV Part II. This form is required by the Securities and Exchange Commission (SEC) or the state of domicile of all investment advisors. In addition, all investment advisors are required to provide this document to prospects before any services are provided. If you are not given one, be sure to ask for it.

# Making Sense of Financial Designations

The investment field has become an alphabet soup, so to speak, of professional designations. Most advisors obtain these designations for two reasons: to set themselves apart from everyone else and to gain the education needed to move their business forward. When searching for professional help, you should place significant emphasis on advisors who have earned the right to use one or more of the following foremost designations. They are ranked in no particular order. I am not suggesting that an advisor with any of the designations is more qualified than an advisor without designations. As in all areas of business, experience counts for a lot.

### Registered Investment Advisor (RIA)

The term *RIA* technically describes an investment firm rather than a particular individual. These firms generally charge a percentage fee that is based on the market value of the assets in your portfolio. To be designated a Registered Investment Advisor, a firm must register with either the Securities and Exchange Commission or their state of domicile.

### Certified Financial Planner (CFP)

The CFP designation is one of the most recognizable and most prestigious designations that a professional advisor can obtain. Professionals with the CFP designation are well grounded in all aspects of financial planning. Areas of investing that the CFP specializes in include investment planning, estate planning, income tax planning, insurance and risk management, retirement planning, and general financial planning. The CFP certificant, as they are called, must pass a number of exams, accumulate three years of related work experience, and complete ongoing continuing education to qualify for the designation.

## Certified Fund Specialist (CFS)

The CFS designation provides a way for advisors to focus their business on mutual funds. Applicants must pass an exam on such topics as investment companies, performance measurement, and asset allocation. Similar to the CFP, the CFS designation requires holders to complete ongoing continuing education credits.

## Certified Public Accountant (CPA)

The CPA designation is one of the most recognizable designations and one of the hardest to obtain. In addition to earning accounting college credits, applicants are required to accumulate two years of work experience and pass a comprehensive exam. The focus of CPAs is geared toward tax preparation, although more and more CPAs are entering the financial and investment planning fields.

## Personal Financial Specialist (PFS)

CPAs who wish to concentrate specifically on financial planning have the opportunity to obtain the PFS designation. This designation is awarded only to CPAs in good standing with the American Institute of Certified Public Accountants (AICPA). This designation covers topics such as estate planning, budgeting and saving, managing credit, and retirement planning.

## Chartered Financial Analyst (CFA)

Along with the CPA designation, the CFA may be perhaps the most difficult designation to earn. I can personally attest to its difficulty. The CFA applicant must pass three rigorous examinations and accumulate three years of professional work experience in the investment field. The CFA is a common designation for investment counselors, portfolio managers, mutual fund managers, and investment analysts.

## Chartered Investment Counselor (CIC)

CFA designation holders who wish to demonstrate their knowledge and extensive work experience have the option of earning the CIC designation. CIC applicants must first obtain the CFA designation, be employed by a member firm of the Investment Counsel Association of America (ICAA), and must have at least five cumulative years of investment work experience.

## Chartered Financial Consultant (ChFC)

The ChFC is very similar in focus to the CFP. The ChFC demonstrates broad knowledge of the financial planning field, such as estate planning, insurance, and investment planning. Similar to CFPs, applicants must accumulate a specific amount of work experience before earning this designation.

## Chartered Life Underwriter (CLU)

The CLU designation is targeted to insurance professionals. Contrary to its name, the CLU is not limited to only life insurance professionals. Many other professionals not employed in the life insurance field have earned the right to use it. Applicants for the CLU designation must complete a 10-course curriculum.

## Chartered Mutual Fund Counselor (CMFC)

Similar to the CFS, the CMFC is a designation tailored to those who work with mutual funds. To obtain this designation, CMFC applicants must complete a self-study program and final examination on various mutual fund topics.

# Resources for Additional Advice

## Recommended Reading

*Getting Started in Asset Allocation* by Eric Gelb and William Bresnan. How to build sensible portfolios for novice investors.

*Global Asset Allocation: Techniques for Optimizing Portfolio Management* by Jess Lederman and Robert Klein. An extensive discussion of asset allocation from the viewpoint of global investing.

*Global Asset Allocation: New Methods and Applications* by Heinz Zimmermann, Peter Oertmann, and Wolfgang Drobetz. Global asset allocation from a theory point of view.

*Strategic Asset Allocation* by John Y. Campbell and Luis M. Viceira. Asset allocation information on the strategy for managing a portfolio.

*Advanced Theory and Methodology of Tactical Asset Allocation* by Wai Lee. A guide to the other asset allocation strategy—tactical asset allocation.

*The Intelligent Asset Allocator* by William Bernstein. A solid presentation on asset allocation with a strong mathematical emphasis.

*Asset Allocation: Balancing Financial Risk* by Roger Gibson. Excellent book covering both the fundamentals and use of asset allocation. Targeted to the financial advisor.

*Efficient Asset Management by* Richard O. Michaud. A book covering how to keep a portfolio's asset mix fully optimized.

*Common Sense on Mutual Funds* by John C. Bogle and Peter L. Bernstein. Terrific work discussing passive investing using a simple approach.

*A Random Walk Down Wall Street* by Burton G. Malkiel. A time-honored book on investing and market behavior.

*Optimal Investing: How to Protect and Grow Your Wealth with Asset Allocation* by Scott P. Frush. Beginners' book for using asset allocation to build an optimal portfolio.

*All About Asset Allocation* by Richard Ferri. A solid book on asset allocation fundamentals and asset classes for novice and intermediate investors.

## Web Sites

*WSJ.com*     A top source, if not the leading source, of broad financial and market information available. A must read on a daily basis.

*iShares.com*     A wealth of information on index funds, specifically exchange-traded funds. Managed by Barclays.

*EfficientFrontier.com*     Terrific Web site for a more theoretical discussion from one of the leading minds and author of books on asset allocation—William Bernstein.

*Morningstar.com*     A good source for the latest market news, investment analysis, and financial happenings. From the company that assigns mutual funds rankings.

*Finance.Yahoo.com*     A personal favorite. An outstanding source for financial information. Covers both the depth and breadth of the market and market participants.

*Bloomberg.com*     Another of my personal favorites. I do not go a day without perusing this leading source of financial news and commentary.

*IndexUniverse.com*     Solid source of information and commentary on increasingly popular and highly beneficial index funds.

*DowJones.com*   Provides an abundant source of historical information for the student of finance and investing. Top source for charting and historical prices.

*Frush.com*   The official Web site of Frush Financial Group, a signature provider of total financial solutions specializing in asset allocation for wealth accumulation and preservation, offers solid financial information and portfolio management services.

## Newspapers and Magazines

*Barron's*
*Bull & Bear Financial Report*
*BusinessWeek*
*The Economist*
*Financial Times*
*Forbes*
*Fortune*
*Kiplinger's Personal Finance*
*Money*
*Mutual Funds*
*Red Herring*
*Smart Money*
*Wall Street Journal*
*Worth*

# Conclusion

I hope you have enjoyed reading *Understanding Asset Allocation* and the easy-to-follow and easy-to-apply strategy for building and managing your portfolio successfully. Hopefully you have learned the importance of asset allocation and now have a better understanding of how to do it properly.

I want to encourage you to continue your commitment to building and protecting your financial independence, control, and security by reviewing this book periodically. If you are interested in learning how my firm can help protect and grow your wealth, please contact us and we will be glad to send you a brochure on our company and the solutions we provide. In addition, please feel free to visit the official author Web site for this book at www.UnderstandingAssetAllocation.com.

Scott Paul Frush, CFA, CFP
Frush Financial Group
37000 Woodward Avenue, Suite 101
Bloomfield Hills, Michigan 48304
Telephone: (248) 642-6800
Fax: (248) 232-1501
E-mail: Contact@Frush.com
www.Frush.com

Be diligent and disciplined in your pursuit to create, grow, and protect your wealth. All the very best in your endeavor!

# Index

197

# About the Author

**Scott Paul Frush, CFA, CFP,** is president of the Frush Financial Group, an investment, tax, and insurance management firm in Bloomfield Hills, Michigan. Frush is an accomplished financial advisor, a portfolio manager, a noted author, and a consultant on asset allocation topics.

Frush has helped people protect, grow, and insure their wealth for more than a decade. In 2002, he founded the Frush Financial Group to manage portfolios for individuals, affluent families, and business pension plans using customized and sophisticated asset allocation solutions. Prior to founding his company, Frush worked at Jay A. Fishman Investment Counsel in Detroit, Michigan, and Stein Roe Mutual Funds in Chicago, Illinois.

Frush earned his Master of Business Administration degree in finance from the University of Notre Dame and his Bachelor of Business Administration degree in finance from Eastern Michigan University, where he currently serves on the alumni association board of directors. He holds the Chartered Financial Analyst (CFA) and Certified Financial Planner (CFP) designations and is insurance licensed for life, health, property, and casualty. Frush is a member of the CFA Institute, Detroit Economic Club, National Association of Tax Professionals, and Global Association of Risk Professionals.

Frush is the author of *Optimal Investing: How to Protect and Grow Your Wealth with Asset Allocation*, published in April 2004, and *Understanding Hedge Funds.* He is also the recipient of two Book of the Year honors for business and investments. In addition, he is the author of two financial booklets: *33 Essential Year-End Financial Tasks* and *17 Secrets of Winning Portfolios.* Frush has been quoted in or his work noted in over 50 publications across the United States.

His firm's management philosophy and investment strategy are based on the topics covered in this book. Frush is presently welcoming new clients. The Frush Financial Group Web site is www.Frush.com.